The AMAZING SPIDER-MAN

The AMAZING SPIDER-MAN

SPIRAL

WRITER:
GERRY CONWAY

PENCILER:
CARLO BARBERI

INKER:
JUAN VLASCO

LETTERER:
VC's JOE CARAMAGNA

COLORIST:
ISRAEL SILVA

COVER ART:
ARTHUR ADAMS & SONIA OBACK (#16.1),
ARTHUR ADAMS & MORRY HOLLOWELL (#17.1)
AND YASMINE PUTRI (#18.1-20.1)

ASSISTANT EDITOR:
DEVIN LEWIS

EDITOR:
NICK LOWE

SPIDER-MAN CREATED BY STAN LEE & STEVE DITKO

Collection Editor: **Jennifer Grünwald**
Assistant Editor: **Sarah Brunstad**
Associate Managing Editor: **Alex Starbuck**
Editor, Special Projects: **Mark D. Beazley**
Senior Editor, Special Projects: **Jeff Youngquist**
SVP Print, Sales & Marketing: **David Gabriel**
Book Designer: **Adam Del Re**

Editor in Chief: **Axel Alonso**
Chief Creative Officer: **Joe Quesada**
Publisher: **Dan Buckley**
Executive Producer: **Alan Fine**

PREVIOUSLY:

*WHEN A MURDEROUS FAMILY OF INTERDIMENSIONAL CREATURES CALLED **THE INHERITORS** BEGAN HUNTING AND FEASTING ON THE LIFEFORCES OF SPIDER-PEOPLE FROM ACROSS THE MULTIVERSE, IT FELL TO PETER PARTKER, **THE AMAZING SPIDER-MAN,** TO LEAD HIS FELLOW SPIDER-MEN AND WOMEN TO VICTORY. NOW HE'S BACK IN NEW YORK CITY AND GETTING BACK TO SPIDEY BASICS!*

AMAZING SPIDER-MAN VOL. 5: SPIRAL. Contains material originally published in magazine form as AMAZING SPIDER-MAN #16.1-20.1. First printing 2015. ISBN# 978-0-7851-9316-6. Published by MARVEL WORLDWIDE, INC., a subsidiary of MARVEL ENTERTAINMENT, LLC. OFFICE OF PUBLICATION: 135 West 50th Street, New York, NY 10020. **Printed in Canada.** ALAN FINE, President, Marvel Entertainment; DAN BUCKLEY, President, TV, Publishing and Brand Management; JOE QUESADA, Chief Creative Officer; TOM BREVOORT, SVP of Publishing; DAVID BOGART, SVP of Operations & Procurement, Publishing; C.B. CEBULSKI, VP of International Development & Brand Management; DAVID GABRIEL, SVP Print, Sales & Marketing; JIM O'KEEFE, VP of Operations & Logistics; DAN CARR, Executive Director of Publishing Technology; SUSAN CRESPI, Editorial Operations Manager; ALEX MORALES, Publishing Operations Manager; STAN LEE, Chairman Emeritus. For information regarding advertising in Marvel Comics or on Marvel.com, please contact Jonathan Rheingold, VP of Custom Solutions & Ad Sales, at jrheingold@marvel.com. For Marvel subscription inquiries, please call 800-217-9158. **Manufactured between 7/31/2015 and 9/7/2015 by SOLISCO PRINTERS, SCOTT, QC, CANADA.**

10 9 8 7 6 5 4 3 2 1

AMAZING SPIDER-MAN 16.1

SPIRAL, PART ONE

AMAZING SPIDER-MAN 16.1 VARIANT
BY SIMONE BIANCHI

I LOVE THIS CITY.
BUT AFTER WHAT'S HAPPENED LATELY--
--THE THINGS I DID, THE OTHER "MANHATTANS" I'VE SEEN--
--IT FEELS... DIFFERENT.
SEE THE EVENTS OF SPIDER-VERSE. --NICK
NO, THAT'S NOT RIGHT.
I FEEL DIFFERENT.
EVERYBODY, TAKE IT DOWN A NOTCH.
OH, GOOD.

JUST WHEN THINGS WERE GETTING DULL AND MOODY.
YOU'RE SERVING A WARRANT, TEDDY. DOESN'T HAVE TO GET UGLY.
TELL IT TO TOMBSTONE, YURI.
POLICE

HE'S THE ONE RAISING AN ARMY. BUILDING AN ARSENAL. GEARING UP FOR A FULL-BLOWN GANG WAR.
SAYS YOUR SOURCE.
THIS ISN'T ONE OF TOMBSTONE'S CONSTRUCTION SITE FRONTS. WE'RE NOT EVEN SURE HE OWNS THIS PLACE.

ARMY? ARSENAL?
GANG WAR?
MORE, PLEASE!
DON'T DO THAT!
MY PEOPLE ARE ON A HAIR TRIGGER. SOMEBODY MIGHT SHOOT YOU.
POLICE

THEY'D MISS.
LOOK, IF THINGS'RE GETTING TENSE, I'D BE HAPPY TO LEND A HAN--
NO!
NO HAND.

BUT, YOU AND ME, ME AND THE WRAITH, WE COULD--
FORGET IT.
WE PLAY THIS BY THE BOOK.

"BY THE BOOK?"
THAT WHAT I TAUGHT YOU?
NEW DAYS, DETECTIVE.
NEW BUREAU CHIEF.
SHE WANTS THE BOOK. WE USE THE BOOK.

MY SOURCE, YURI. MY CALL.
MIGHT BE YOUR SOURCE, TEDDY, BUT IT'S MY PRECINCT. I'M RESPONSIBLE FOR--
CAPTAIN--
TTKK TTKKK TTKKKK
NNGH
TEDDY!
CHNK CHNK
CHNK CHNK

WHO STARTED THIS?
WHO STARTED SHOOTING?
ONE OF THE SWATS--
HE RAISED HIS GUN.
I THOUGHT--

YOU "THOUGHT"?

CRUNCH

TATS!
WHATCHA NEED, BOSS?

NEED YOU TO KILL 'EM!
KILL EVERYBODY!

EVEN BEFORE I TOOK A ROUND TRIP THROUGH THE MULTIVERSE, I ALREADY KNEW FATE WAS A FRAGILE THING.
DOWN! DOWN!
AFTER ALL, I'M NOT JUST YOUR TYPICAL FRIENDLY NEIGHBORHOOD WEB-SPINNER.
I'M A PHYSICIST.
ALTERNATE REALITIES, QUANTUM MECHANICS.
OLD NEWS, RIGHT?
WASN'T SUPPOSED TO BE LIKE THIS.
TAKA KAKAA
I HAD A PLAN!
GOOD FOR YOU, CREW-TOP. PLANS ARE TERRIFIC.
TAKAKA-

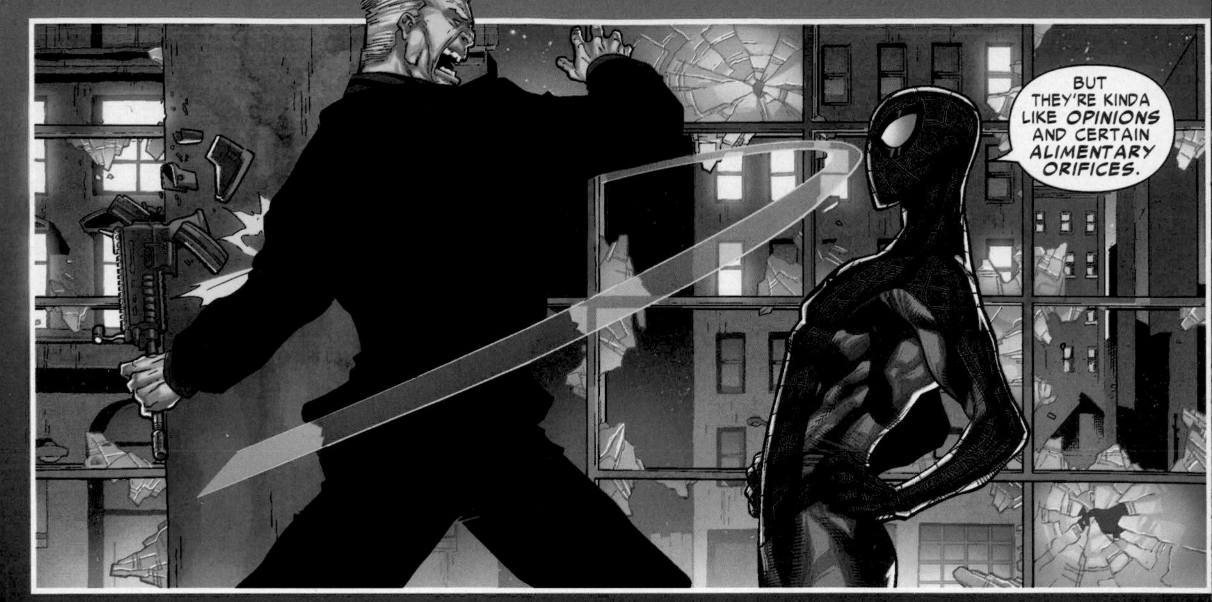
BUT THEY'RE KINDA LIKE *OPINIONS* AND CERTAIN *ALIMENTARY ORIFICES.*

EVERYBODY'S GOT ONE.
NOBODY'S IMPRESSED.

STILL, IT'S *ONE* THING TO ACCEPT THE FRAGILITY OF FATE AND THE POWER OF CHOICE IN THEORY.

COMING MASK TO MASK WITH A DIFFERENT YOU?
THAT IS A HIT TO THE GUT.

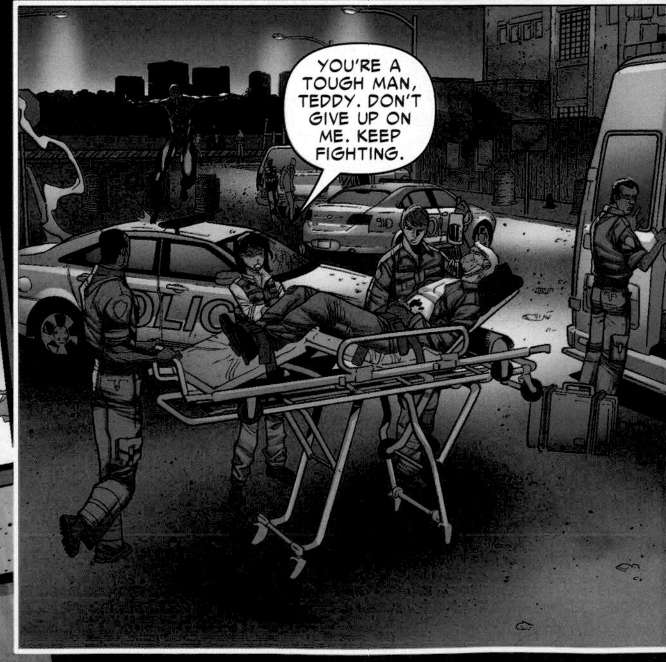
YOU'RE A TOUGH MAN, TEDDY. DON'T GIVE UP ON ME. KEEP FIGHTING.

FRIEND OF YOURS?
MORE THAN A FRIEND. TEDDY RANGEL MENTORED ME MY FIRST YEAR ON THE FORCE. HE HAD MY BACK. HE WAS MY "RABBI."
EVERYTHING I AM TODAY, I OWE TO THAT MAN.
911

BETTER HOPE YOUR BUDDY CHOKES ON A RESPIRATOR, WATANABE.
HE MIXED IN MY BUSINESS, THAT MAKES HIM A DEA--

THWAP
KNGMPH

SORRY ABOUT YOUR FRIEND, CAPTAIN.
WHATEVER HAPPENS TO HIM, IF HE'S ANYTHING LIKE YOU, I BET HE'D SAY IT WAS WORTH IT.
SCORE THIS AS A WIN FOR THE GOOD GUYS.

100 CENTRE STREET, EIGHT DAYS LATER.
...PURSUANT TO THE COURT'S DETERMINATION THAT THE ORIGINAL SEARCH WARRANT WAS DEFECTIVE, ALL CHARGES DERIVED FROM EVIDENCE PRODUCED UNDER AUTHORITY OF SAID WARRANT ARE DISMISSED.
THE COURT ORDERS THE DEFENDANT, LONNIE THOMPSON LINCOLN, TO BE RELEASED FROM CUSTODY.
WHAT?!

PROBLEM, OFFICER?

AH, THE CAPTAIN WAS ADDRESSING ME, JUDGE.
IT'S TRUE WE CAN'T IDENTIFY THE SOURCE DETECTIVE RANGEL REFERENCED IN HIS ORIGINAL WARRANT APPLICATION--

--BUT ONLY BECAUSE OF THE OFFICER'S CURRENT MEDICAL STATUS--
HE'S IN A COMA, JUDGE.

SADLY, POLICE WORK HAS ITS RISKS.
ALL THE MORE REASON TO MAINTAIN LEGALLY SUFFICIENT SUPPORT DOCUMENTATION.
RULING STANDS. CASE DISMISSED.

THIS IS ON YOU, WATANABE.
CHIEF--
FULL AUDIT. DOCUMENT PROTOCOLS. YOUR PRECINCT.
BUT--
MY DESK. TOMORROW. EIGHT A.M.

I WANTED TO *PUNCH* HER.

HERE YOU ARE FIGHTING FOR YOUR LIFE, BUT ALL CHIEF YARBOROUGH WANTS IS TO *AUDIT* MY *PAPERWORK*.
BACK IN THE DAY YOU MADE IT SOUND SO *SIMPLE*.
"A COP HAS TWO JOBS, YURI.
"PROTECT HIS PARTNER. CATCH THE BAD GUYS."
I BLEW BOTH.
UH, CAPTAIN?

MY TEAM'S HERE TO INSTALL A NEW ELECTRICAL SYSTEM--
--SOMETHING PARKER INDUSTRIES WORKED UP DURING THE *ELECTRO* MESS--*
--AND I, *UH*, HEARD ABOUT YOUR FRIEND--
--UMM.
HE OKAY? YOU OKAY?
ASM #1-6. --NICK

HE'S IN A COMA AND I'M *TIRED*, PARKER.
TIRED OF PUSHING THE SAME ROCK UP A HILL OVER AND OVER.
WITH THE *KINGPIN GONE* IN EUROPE, LOCAL GANGS ARE HUNGRY FOR POWER AND TURF.
THE CITY'S A TURKEY DINNER.
MY PRECINCT IS THE CARVING BOARD.

YOU DATED CARLIE COOPER. YOU UNDERSTAND THE LIFE COPS LEAD.
A GOOD MAN LIKE TEDDY RANGEL RISKS EVERYTHING TO PROTECT THIS CITY, AND FOR WHAT?
SO SOME THICK-HEADED JUDICIAL *PARASITE* CAN THROW IT ALL AWAY?
BUT THAT'S THE DEAL, RIGHT?
YOU DO WHAT YOU DO, BUT YOU PLAY BY THE RULES.
OTHERWISE YOU END UP CROSSING LINES YOU SHOULD *NEVER* CROSS.
GOING PLACES YOU SHOULDN'T GO.
THAT'S WHAT WE TELL OURSELVES.
BUT SOMETIMES I WONDER--
CODE BLUE!
WE NEED A CRASH CART!

IT WAS ME, YOU KNOW.
I WAS TEDDY'S SOURCE.
MARTIN LI...
CAPTAIN WATANABE, WE BOTH KNOW MARTIN LI BARELY EXISTS. MY FRIENDS CALL ME MISTER NEGATIVE.
SO DO MY ENEMIES.
ON THE WHOLE, I'D PREFER WE WERE FRIENDS.
DON'T TOUCH ME.
AFRAID I'LL CORRUPT YOU?
NOT MY INTENTION, CAPTAIN.
WE SHARE CERTAIN... INTERESTS. YOU MIGHT FIND THIS USEFUL.

WHERE'D YOU GET THESE?
MY INNER DEMONS HAVE REMARKABLE ACCESS.
YOU DO REALIZE WHAT YOU'RE LOOKING AT?
JUDGE HOWELL...RECEIVING ILLEGAL DRUGS FROM...THAT'S ONE OF TOMBSTONE'S GUYS...
HYDROCODONE
I KNOW WHY YOU'RE DOING THIS.
TIPPING OFF DETECTIVE RANGEL--NOW, THESE PHOTOS--
IT'S A TAKEOVER PLAY.
OBVIOUSLY.
THE QUESTION YOU NEED TO ASK YOURSELF, CAPTAIN, IS--
DO YOU CARE?
CHIEF!

COULD BE FAKE. HAVE THE LAB LOOK AT THEM.
RIGHT. SURE.
MEANTIME, ABOUT THE WARRANT. WE CAN'T ALERT--

WHAT WARRANT?
TO ARREST JUDGE HOWELL. WE HAVE TO--

ARREST HOWELL? ON WHAT CHARGE?
COLLUSION-- CONSPIRACY--
TOMBSTONE IS HIS *DRUG DEALER*.

NONSENSE. YOU CAN'T PROVE THAT.
BUT THESE PHOTOS--

--SHOW TOMBSTONE'S MAN GIVING HOWELL A BOTTLE.
DOES IT CONTAIN DRUGS? HOW DO WE KNOW?
HOW DO WE KNOW *TOMBSTONE* IS PART OF IT?

FOLLOW PROCEDURE. DO YOUR PAPERWORK. WE HAVE RULES, CAPTAIN.
WE'RE COPS. NOT *VIGILANTES*.

CALL 911
MAYBE THAT'S THE PROBLEM.

I'VE BEEN TRYING TOO HARD TO FOLLOW THE RULES.

I BECAME *THE WRAITH* BECAUSE FOLLOWING THE RULES WASN'T GOOD ENOUGH.
I QUIT AFTER CARLIE DISCOVERED MY SECRET BUT PROMISED NOT TO TURN ME IN.
San
ASM VOL. 1, #664. --NICK.

I ONLY TOOK THE MASK AGAIN TO HELP HER EXPOSE DOC OCK'S CONNECTION TO SPIDER-MAN'S STRANGE BEHAVIOR A FEW MONTHS AGO.
TOLD IN THE EPIC SUPERIOR SPIDER-MAN. --NICK

SINCE THEN I'VE STRUGGLED TO FIND MY WAY BACK TO BEING A "GOOD COP."
BUT BEING A "GOOD COP" GOT MY FRIEND KILLED AND SET TOMBSTONE FREE.
TIME FOR PLAN B.

THIS IS WHERE I'M SUPPOSED TO MAKE A SPEECH ABOUT NOT LETTING YOUR ANGER OVER DETECTIVE RANGEL'S DEATH TRICK YOU INTO DOING SOMETHING STUPID.
BECAUSE WHEN YOU THINK ABOUT IT--
--DOING SOMETHING STUPID IS KINDA *MY* GIG.

TOMBSTONE IS DEALING DRUGS FROM THIS CONSTRUCTION SITE.
ONE OF HIS CUSTOMERS IS JUDGE HOWELL.
SERIOUSLY? YOU CAN PROVE THAT?

IF I COULD, I'D BE HERE WITH A SWAT TEAM.
SO WE'RE LOOKING FOR--?
EVIDENCE.
DRUGS. RECORDS.
ANYTHING THAT TIES TOMBSTONE TO HOWELL.

MAYBE THAT *VAULT* OVER THERE?
IS THIS A PERSONAL THING FOR YOU?
OH, IT'S *PERSONAL*.
JUST ASKING.

YOUGOTTABEKIDDINGME.
WHO KEEPS AN ANTI-TANK LAUNCHER ON A CONSTRUCTION SITE?
SWOOSH
NOT GOOD, NOT GOOD, NOT GOOD--
GO!

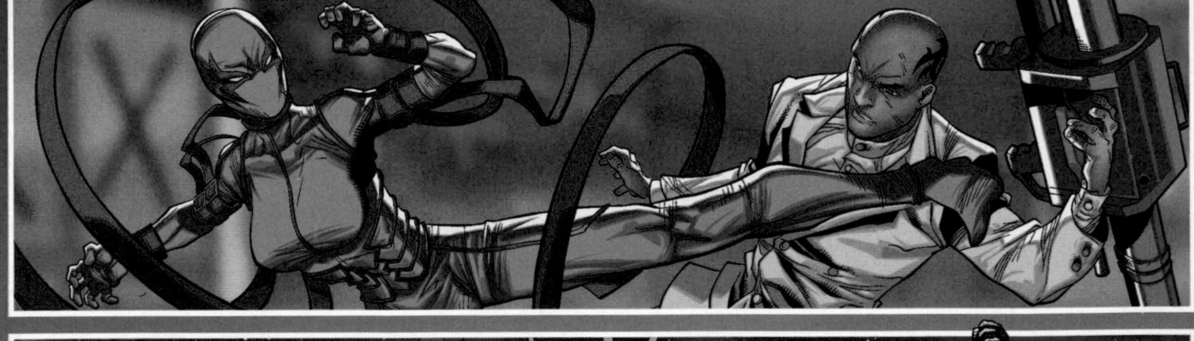

REALLY NOT GOOD.

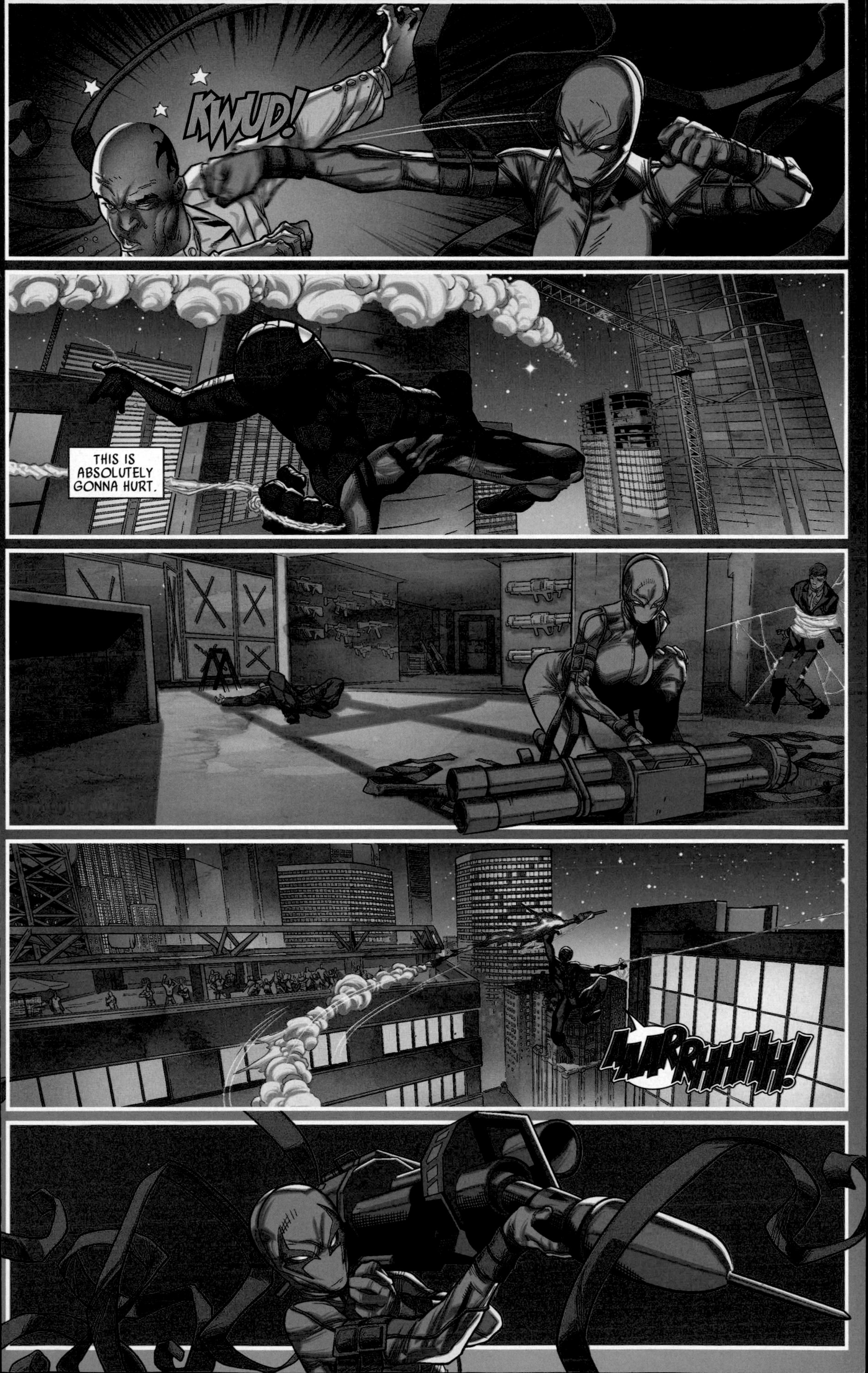
KWUD!
THIS IS ABSOLUTELY GONNA HURT.
AAARRHHHH!

WELL, THAT WORKED OUT.
ALWAYS BETTER WHEN MISSILES DON'T GO BOOM IN MIDTOWN.

BOOM

WHAT DID YOU DO?
WHAT NEEDED TO BE DONE.

YOU BLEW OPEN A VAULT WITH AN ANTI-TANK MISSILE!
YOU COULD'VE KILLED SOMEBODY!
TOMBSTONE.
HE WAS HIDING IN THE VAULT. I COULD'VE KILLED TOMBSTONE.
BUT I DIDN'T.

(THOUGH HE MAY NEED A HEARING AID WHILE HE BEGS HIS LAWYER TO GET HIM A PLEA BARGAIN.)
THAT'S NOT THE POINT!
YOU'RE A COP!

GOT IT.
TOMBSTONE KEPT A LEDGER OF ALL HIS DRUG DEALS.
IF HOWELL'S NAME IS IN HERE--

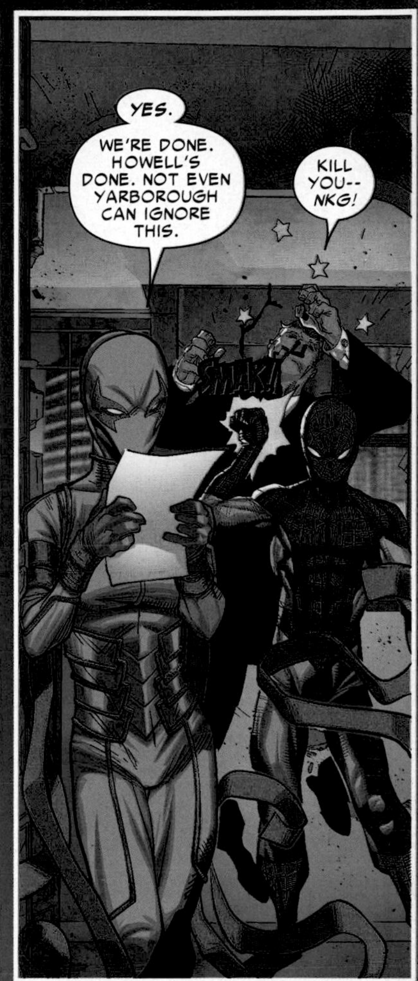

YES.
WE'RE DONE. HOWELL'S DONE. NOT EVEN YARBOROUGH CAN IGNORE THIS.
KILL YOU--NKG!
SMAK!!

I DON'T THINK YOU SEE THE PROBLEM HERE.
COPS AREN'T SUPPOSED TO BLOW THINGS UP!
YOU DON'T SEE.

WATANABE IS THE COP.

I'M THE WRAITH.
CHOICES MATTER. FATE IS FRAGILE.
I KNOW BECAUSE I'M NOT JUST A PHYSICIST.
I'M YOUR TYPICAL FRIENDLY NEIGHBORHOOD WEB-SPINNER.
AND I HAVE A VERY BAD FEELING YURI WATANABE JUST MADE A VERY BAD CHOICE.

AMAZING SPIDER-MAN 17.1 VARAINT
BY GABRIELE DELL'OTTO

AMAZING SPIDER-MAN 17.1

SPIRAL, PART TWO

Uptown Manhattan.
THE "STARLIGHT BALLROOM" AT THE HOTEL KNICKERBOCKER...
THE SIMPLICITY OF THE THING IS WHAT I FIND APPEALING.
NO DRAWN-OUT NEGOTIATIONS, NO WASTED MANPOWER. NO FUSS, NO DRAMA.
WE SETTLE OUR DIFFERENCES LIKE ADULTS.
WE PUT YOUR CHALLENGER IN THE CAGE WITH MY GUY, SCRATCH.
"TWO GO IN..."

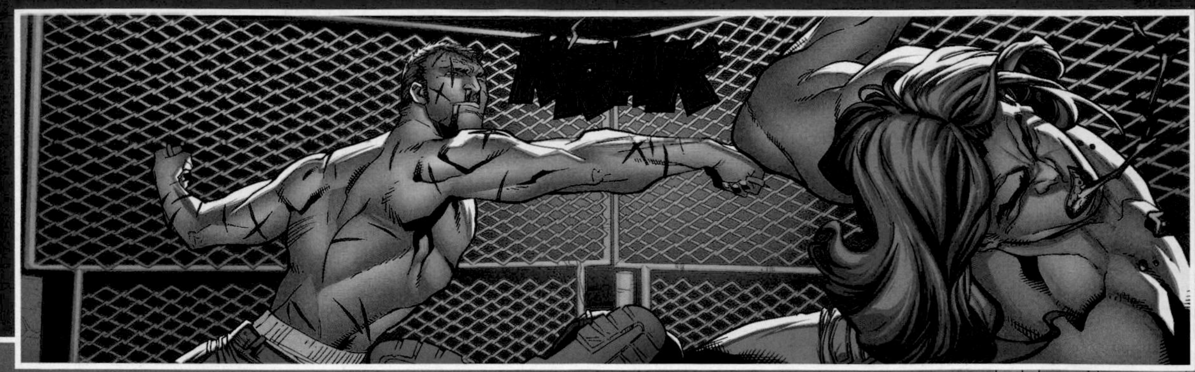

...ONE COMES OUT.
AND WINNER TAKES ALL?

LIKE I SAY, IT'S THE SIMPLICITY OF THE THING THAT APPEALS TO ME.
ME, TOO.
DEAL.

HNNH?
YOU'RE OKAY WITH THIS?
I'M NOT CRAZY LIKE MY PREDECESSOR, HAMMERHEAD.
THIS GOBLIN KING KNOWS A GOOD BUSINESS PROPOSITION WHEN HE HEARS ONE.
JUST ONE THING--

WE FIGHT ON NEUTRAL GROUND. NOT HERE.
AGREED. WE'RE COMPETING FOR TOMBSTONE'S TERRITORY--
I'LL FIND US A VENUE IN THE THIRD PRECINCT.

GOOD ENOUGH. NOW ALL WE NEED--
WHAT?
WHAT ARE YOU--?
SKRASH

THE PROBLEM WITH SECRET GANGLAND MEETINGS HELD IN *ROOFTOP* BALLROOMS?
ANYBODY SWINGING BY ON A WEB LINE CAN SEE YOU DOING BUSINESS.
SLOPPY SECURITY, GUYS.
IF THE *KINGPIN* WERE STILL AROUND HE'D SLAP YOU SILLY.
YOU KNOW HOW TO REACH ME, HAMMERHEAD.

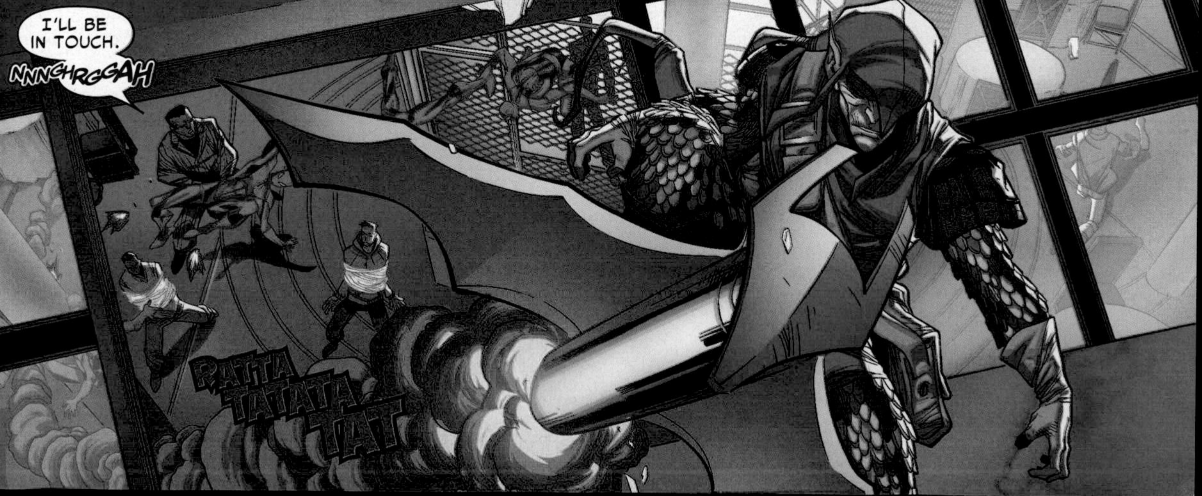
I'LL BE IN TOUCH.
NNNGHRGGAH
RATTA TATATA TAT

TOMMY GUNS IN THE 21ST CENTURY? RETRO IS SO RETRO.
YOU WANT TO SHOOT THINGS, HAMMY.
--TAKE A TIP FROM THE FRANK CASTLE MANIAC PLAYBOOK AND GET YOURSELF A REAL WEAPON.
GRRNNGH
OR, HEY, JUST A THOUGHT--
GO THE MENTAL HEALTH ROUTE AND TRY SOME ANGER MANAGEMENT.
KONK
SIGH.
SERIOUSLY?

SOMETIMES IT FEELS LIKE I'M TALKING TO MYSELF.

BEFORE I DROPPED IN I HEARD HAMMERHEAD TALK ABOUT FINDING A "VENUE" SOMEWHERE IN TOMBSTONE'S OLD TURF.
YOU KNOW WHAT'S UP WITH THAT?
NNGH
I'M GUESSING PROBABLY NOT.
TOMBSTONE'S TURF WAS IN THE THIRD PRECINCT.

THE THIRD IS YURI WATANABE'S PRECINCT.
THAT MEANS HER PRECINCT IS STILL CENTER STAGE IN NEW YORK'S ONGOING GANG WAR.
GOOD.
THE WAY SHE WENT OFF THE RAILS AS THE WRAITH A FEW NIGHTS AGO...*
ASM 16.1 --NICK.

...SHE AND I ARE DUE FOR A HEART-TO-HEART ANYWAY.
I COULD HAVE YOU SUSPENDED, WATANABE.
YOU DISOBEYED A DIRECT ORDER.
ALL DUE RESPECT, CHIEF--

--YOU ASKED ME TO HAVE THE LAB AUTHENTICATE THESE PHOTOS OF JUDGE HOWELL BUYING DRUGS FROM TOMBSTONE'S RIGHTHAND MAN.
THAT'S WHAT I DID.

YOU ALSO *ARRESTED* HOWELL.
WITHOUT WAITING FOR CSI'S REPORT.
THAT WAS THE D.A.'S CALL.
BASED ON EVIDENCE *YOU* PROVIDED.

WE RECEIVED A LEDGER IN TOMBSTONE'S HANDWRITING.
IT CONFIRMED HOWELL WAS A CUSTOMER FOR ILLICIT PHARMACEUTICALS.
THIS *LEDGER*...
IT CAME FROM THE SAME *ANONYMOUS* SOURCE WHO PROVIDED THOSE PHOTOS?

NO.

WE HAVE *PROCEDURES* TO DEAL WITH UNSOURCED EVIDENCE AND ANONYMOUS TIPS, CAPTAIN.
YOU IGNORED THEM.
I GOT RESULTS.

YOU GOT *REVENGE*.

BY THE WAY...
...JUDGE HOWELL ASKED TO SEE YOU.
ME?
WHY?

ASK HIM YOURSELF.
HE'S ON RYKER'S.
CITY OF NEW YORK CORRECTION DEPARTMENT RYKERS ISLAND HOME OF NEW YORKS BOLDEST
"BUT YOU KNOW THAT...

"YOU PUT HIM THERE."

THUMP
SHI--

WHOA.
SOMEBODY'S A BIT TETCHY.
WHAT DO YOU THINK YOU'RE DOING?

WARNING A FRIEND.
HAMMERHEAD AND THE GOBLIN KING HAD A MEET LAST NIGHT.

ABOUT WHAT?

DON'T KNOW, BUT YOUR PRECINCT WAS A HOT TOPIC.
FIGURES.
JAILING TOMBSTONE CREATED A LOCAL POWER VACUUM.
WITH KINGPIN GONE, THUGS LIKE THOSE TWO WILL TRY TO FILL IT.

RIGHT. ABOUT TOMBSTONE. HOW YOU HANDLED HIM THE OTHER NIGHT--
THINK MAYBE YOU WERE A LITTLE, AH, OVER-ENTHUSIASTIC?
HE KILLED MY FRIEND.

HEY, I KNOW HOW YOU FEEL, BELIEVE ME, BETTER THAN YOU CAN IMAGINE.
BUT WE CAN'T MAKE THIS PERSONAL.
I LEARNED THAT A LONG TIME AGO.

WE CATCH THE BAD GUYS AND LET THE SYSTEM DO THE REST.
"THE SYSTEM"?
"THE SYSTEM" RUN BY IDIOT PAPER PUSHERS LIKE MY CHIEF AND CORRUPT JUDGES LIKE ANSON HOWELL?

SEE FOR YOURSELF. "THE SYSTEM" IS A JOKE.
IT ALWAYS WAS.

"I'M JUST NOT LAUGHING ANYMORE."

Downtown Manhattan.
FUTURE SITE OF YET ANOTHER FIFTY-STORY CONDOMINIUM DEDICATED TO THE HOUSING NEEDS OF THE ONE PERCENT...
PERFECT.

GET WORD TO GOBLIN KING WE'LL BE READY BY MIDNIGHT.
SURE ABOUT THIS, BOSS?

WHY WOULDN'T I BE SURE?
WELL, UH, WITH SCRATCH IN JAIL--WHO'S GONNA FIGHT FOR OUR SIDE?

HEH.

TONIGHT. MIDNIGHT.
YES.
AS YOU EXPECTED.

Ryker's Island State Penitentiary.
CAPTAIN WATANABE, I HAVE A CONFESSION TO MAKE.
REALLY?
SHOULD I CALL THE D.A.?
SHE'LL BE HAPPY TO TAKE A PLEA.

YES, I BOUGHT DRUGS FROM TOMBSTONE--PAINKILLERS--FOR MY WIFE.
THREE YEARS AGO SURGEONS REMOVED A TUMOR FROM HER SPINE.

EVER SINCE SHE'S BEEN IN CONSTANT, UNREMITTING AGONY.
CAN YOU IMAGINE WHAT THAT'S LIKE, CAPTAIN?

WATCHING SOMEONE YOU LOVE DIE A LITTLE EVERY DAY?
IT'S A HORROR.

THE MEDICATIONS PRESCRIBED FOR LINDSEY WERE NEVER ENOUGH.
SHE NEEDED MORE.
SO YOU MADE A DEAL.
TOMBSTONE GAVE YOU WHAT YOU WANTED FOR YOUR WIFE.
AND YOU LET HIM WALK.

NO!
YES, I BOUGHT DRUGS--
--I ADMIT THAT CRIME--
BUT THAT'S ALL I DID. I SWEAR!
I HAD NO IDEA TOMBSTONE WAS INVOLVED!
YOU *VACATED* DETECTIVE RANGEL'S SEARCH WARRANT.

BECAUSE IT WAS *DEFECTIVE!*
DETECTIVE RANGEL MADE A MISTAKE.
THE LAW IS CLEAR, THERE ARE PRECEDENTS, WE HAVE A *SYSTEM*--

DON'T TALK TO ME ABOUT YOUR SYSTEM!

CAPTAIN.
PLEASE.
I'VE HEARD...FROM OTHER INMATES... TOMBSTONE THINKS I'M A *DANGER* TO HIM.

IF YOU DON'T DROP THE *COLLUSION* CHARGE, HE MIGHT KILL ME.

HONESTLY, YOUR HONOR?
I DON'T SEE A PROBLEM.

I HAVE ANOTHER TIP FOR YOU, CAPTAIN.
BETTER THAN THE PHOTOS OF HOWELL BUYING DRUGS FROM TOMBSTONE'S SECOND-IN-COMMAND?

BECAUSE IF IT HADN'T BEEN FOR *THE WRAITH* AND *SPIDER-MAN*, THAT TIP WOULD'VE LED NOWHERE.
HAMMERHEAD AND THE GOBLIN KING ARE PLANNING A MATCH FIGHT TO SETTLE WHO'LL TAKE OVER TOMBSTONE'S TURF.

MIDNIGHT TONIGHT AT THE OLD *EMPIRE ROYALE* IN THE DOWNTOWN THEATER DISTRICT.
THANKS.

"THANKS"? AREN'T YOU THE LEAST BIT CONCERNED I MIGHT BE *PLAYING* YOU, CAPTAIN?
EVERYBODY PLAYS EVERYBODY, "MR. NEGATIVE."

WHY SHOULD YOU AND I BE ANY DIFFERENT?
I KNOW WHAT YURI WATANABE IS GOING THROUGH.

I FELT THE SAME WAY AFTER UNCLE BEN DIED.
THEN, AFTER WHAT HAPPENED TO GWEN--
WELL, IT TOOK ME A LONG TIME TO THINK STRAIGHT.
I BLAMED MYSELF FOR UNCLE BEN'S DEATH.
I BLAMED MYSELF FOR GWEN'S.
BUT NOBODY CAN LIVE WITH THAT KIND OF GUILT.
SO YOU TURN IT OUTWARD.
YOU FIND OTHERS TO SHARE THE BLAME.
THAT'S WHEN YOUR LIFE GETS DARK.
BECAUSE THE GUILT NEVER REALLY GOES AWAY...
...AND THERE'S ALWAYS SOMEBODY NEW TO BLAME.

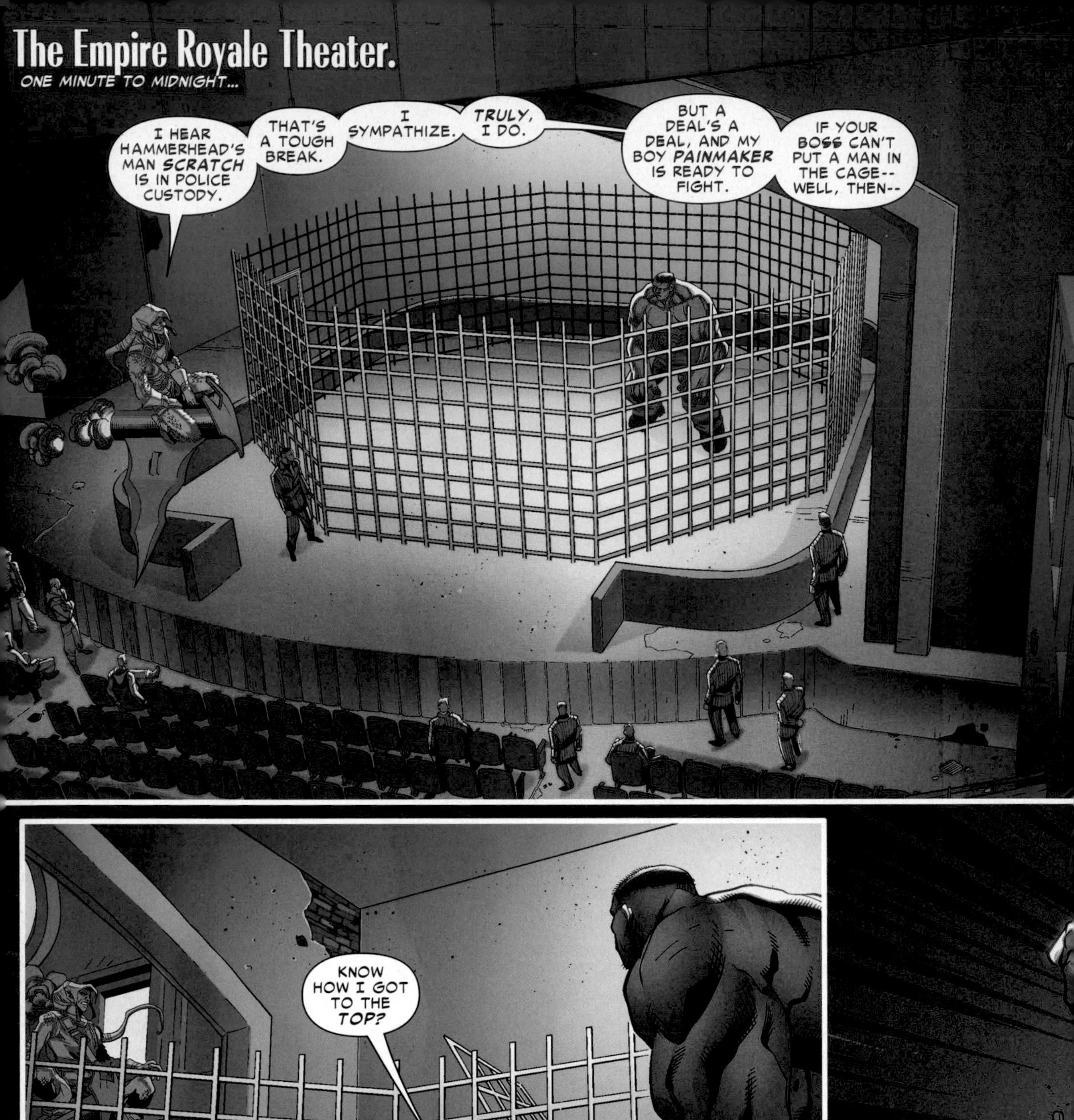
The Empire Royale Theater.
ONE MINUTE TO MIDNIGHT...
I HEAR HAMMERHEAD'S MAN SCRATCH IS IN POLICE CUSTODY.
THAT'S A TOUGH BREAK.
I SYMPATHIZE.
TRULY, I DO.
BUT A DEAL'S A DEAL, AND MY BOY PAINMAKER IS READY TO FIGHT.
IF YOUR BOSS CAN'T PUT A MAN IN THE CAGE-- WELL, THEN--

KNOW HOW I GOT TO THE TOP?

WHO SAID I CAN'T PUT A MAN IN THE CAGE?
BEFORE I RAN MY OWN GANG I WAS A MAGGIA ENFORCER.
HEAD FIRST!

OH.
MY.
GOD.
GNGNGNH
ANY QUESTIONS?
TINK
TINK
TINK

I HAVE A QUESTION.
WHAT MAKES EITHER OF YOU THINK YOU CAN USE MY TERRITORY AS A KILLING GROUND FOR YOUR PATHETIC TURF WARS?

I SEE WHAT YOU DID THERE.
CLAIMING THE THIRD PRECINCT AS WRAITH-PROTECTED TERRITORY.
NICE PLOY.

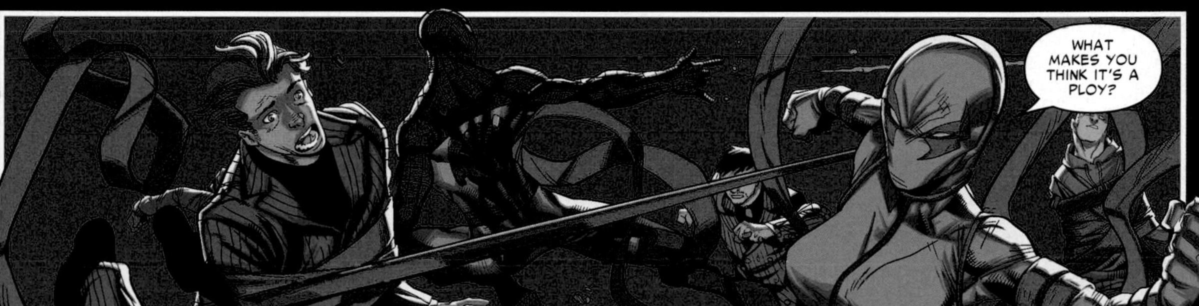
WHAT MAKES YOU THINK IT'S A PLOY?

WE DON'T HAVE TERRITORY.

WHAT MAKES YOU THINK THERE'S A "WE"?

BUT I THOUGHT--

I'VE BEEN WAITING FOR A CHANCE LIKE THIS.
ALWAYS WANTED TO GET YOU SOMEWHERE NICE N' TIGHT WHERE YOU COULDN'T JUMP AROUND.
JUST THE TWO OF US--

UP CLOSE.
RGNGNH
PERSONAL!
KRUNCH
HNGNGR
PEOPLE LIKE YOU, PEOPLE LIKE GOBLIN KING, KNOW WHAT YOUR PROBLEM IS?
YOU SEE A GUY LIKE ME--I WEAR A SUIT, I CARRY A GUN, I RUN A CREW, I'VE GOT A PLATE IN MY HEAD.
YOU THINK YOU KNOW ME.
YOU DON'T KNOW ME!
YOU'RE RIGHT.

SOMETIMES I WONDER IF YOU CAN EVER REALLY KNOW *ANYONE*.
HEY--
GOBLIN KING GOT AWAY.
AFTER THE WAY WE CLEANED UP HIS MEN, I DOUBT HE'LL BE BACK.
I THINK HE GOT THE *MESSAGE*.
YEAH?
WHAT MESSAGE IS THAT, YURI?
WE DON'T PROTECT "TURF"--WE PROTECT PEOPLE, WE CATCH BAD GUYS.
THERE HAS TO BE A *DIFFERENCE* BETWEEN WHAT WE DO AND WHAT *THEY* DO.

YOU WORRY ABOUT THE DIFFERENCE. I'LL WORRY ABOUT RESULTS.
I WORRY ABOUT YOU.
I LOOKED AT THOSE PHOTOS IN JUDGE HOWELL'S EVIDENCE FILE.
IT'S OBVIOUS THEY WERE TAKEN BY SOMEBODY INSIDE TOMBSTONE'S CREW.

SO?
SO THAT MEANS HOWELL AND TOMBSTONE WERE SET UP.
SOMEBODY USED HOWELL TO PUT TOMBSTONE IN JAIL.

SO?

I WAS WRONG.
I TOLD YURI I KNEW HOW SHE FELT.
I THOUGHT I UNDERSTOOD THE DARK PLACE THOSE FEELINGS CAN LEAD TO.
I'M STARTING TO THINK THAT I HAVE NO IDEA.

AMAZING SPIDER-MAN 18.1 VARIANT
BY GREG LAND & MORRY HOLLOWELL

AMAZING SPIDER-MAN 18.1

SPIRAL, PART THREE

Manhattan's Third Precinct.
AN UNDEVELOPED SECTION OF THE WEST SIDE'S HIGH LINE...
2:00 A.M.
GIVE YOU THIS, SPECS.
YOU SHOW SERIOUS WEIGHT, TURNING UP ON HAMMERHEAD'S STREETS--
--MAKING A GRAB FOR OUR TURF--
--WHILE YOUR BOSS WARMS A COT ON RYKER'S.
KANG
DOESN'T MATTER WHERE THE MAN TUCKS HIS HEAD.
TOMBSTONE SAYS TAKE YOUR TURF--

--WE TAKE YOUR TURF.
KRUNCH
BOYS, BOYS.
AS AMUSING AS IT MAY BE TO WATCH YOU BEAT EACH OTHER TO A PULP--
--LET ME OFFER AN *ALTERNATIVE* TO MUTUALLY ASSURED SELF-DESTRUCTION.
PUT YOUR TOYS AWAY--

--EASE BACK ON THE *TESTOSTERONE*--

WHAK
--AND LET A WOMAN TAKE CHARGE.
AND BY "WOMAN," OBVIOUSLY I MEAN ME:
THE BLACK CAT.
SO?
THIS IS THE PART WHERE YOU FALL ALL OVER EACH OTHER TO ACCEPT THE INEVITABLE AND SWEAR UNDYING LOYALTY.
WHO WANTS TO GO FIRST?
NEVER GONNA HAPPEN
FORGET IT
NO WAY
BITE
EAT
TOMBSTON
HAMMERHEAD
OWE HIM
OWE 'IM
HAMMERHEAD
TOMBSTONE
WE A CREW.
CREW WORKS FOR ONE MAN.
THAT'S WHY IT'S A CREW.
CALL IT RESPECT.
TILL HE SAYS OTHERWISE--
--WE WORK FOR HIM. NOBODY ELSE.

HUH.

THAT'S DISAPPOINTING.
YES. TOMBSTONE AND HAMMERHEAD INSPIRE FIERCE LOYALTY.
TOUGH TO COUNTER, BUT NOT IMPOSSIBLE.

CRIME MASTER?
I KNOW-- YOU THOUGHT I WAS DEAD.
THAT WAS MY PREDECESSOR.
SAME MASK, SAME NAME--NEW MODEL.
I BELIEVE YOU'VE MET A FEW OF MY COLLEAGUES--

THE OX AND SNAKE MARSTON, FORMERLY OF THE THUNDERBOLTS--
THINGS THERE DIDN'T WORK OUT.
CREATIVE DIFFERENCES.
HAMMER HARRISON, ONE OF THE FEW MEN TO LAND CONSECUTIVE HITS ON SPIDER-MAN--
PEOPLE SAY I'M GOOD WITH MY HANDS.
AND, OF COURSE, FANCY DAN, AN EARLY FOUNDER OF THIS TROOP KNOWN COLLECTIVELY AS--THE ENFORCERS.
MA'AM.
MAY I SAY, IT WAS A PLEASURE TO WATCH YOU WORK.
YOU ARE POETRY IN MOTION.

UH... THANKS?
YOU WONDER WHY WE'RE HERE.
NOT TO COMPETE, I ASSURE YOU.
TO ASSIST.

ASSIST HOW?
WITH KINGPIN OUT OF THE PICTURE, THE CRIMINAL ELEMENT OF THIS CITY DEMANDS NEW LEADERSHIP.
I'VE WATCHED YOU RISE, CAT.

YOU CAN PROVIDE THAT LEADERSHIP.
YOU HAVE THE SKILLS AND THE CHARISMA.
ALL YOU NEED IS A PLAN.

COLOR ME INTRIGUED.
HAMMERHEAD AND TOMBSTONE COMMAND THE UNBREAKABLE LOYALTY OF THEIR MEN.
DON'T TRY TO BREAK THAT LOYALTY.

CO-OPT IT.
MAKE TOMBSTONE AND HAMMERHEAD LOYAL TO YOU.
HOW DO I DO THAT?

WITH OUR HELP--
I SUGGEST AN OLD-SCHOOL JAILBREAK.

11:00 A.M.
Parker Industries.
...AND THAT'S WHY I RECOMMEND WE INFLATE THE FRAMISTAN WITH THE BLAG-BARTER BEFORE THE WHIZ-KICKER FRETS THE ODOMETER.

HM? RIGHT.
SOUNDS GOOD.
SO YOU'RE NOT WORRIED WE'LL PUT TOO MUCH FLANG IN THE SPANG?

NOPE.
WHATEVER YOU DECIDE IS FINE BY ME.
PETER!
I'M BABBLING NONSENSE!

WHAT?
I'VE BEEN TRYING TO HAVE A CONVERSATION WITH YOU BUT YOU'RE LOST IN YOUR OWN HEAD.
TALK TO ME.

SORRY.
I'M WORRIED ABOUT A FRIEND.
SHE'S MADE SOME... REALLY POOR DECISIONS LATELY.
ANNA MARIA...DO YOU THINK GOOD PEOPLE CAN GO BAD?

YOU'RE TALKING TO A WOMAN WHO FELL IN LOVE WITH A GUY WHO HIJACKED ANOTHER GUY'S BODY.

OTTO MADE A LOT OF POOR DECISIONS.
IN THE END HE MADE SOME GOOD ONES, TOO.

WAS HE A *GOOD* MAN WHO DID *BAD* THINGS, A *BAD* MAN WHO DID *GOOD* THINGS, OR A BIT OF *BOTH?*
I WISH I KNEW.

THE DIFFERENCE BETWEEN OTTO AND YOUR FRIEND IS...
...*HE* CAN'T SETTLE THE ISSUE.
SHE CAN.
5:25 P.M.
HUDSON STREET, HOME OF MANHATTAN'S THIRD PRECINCT.
THIS WON'T BE FUN.
YURI WATANABE DIDN'T FIGHT HER WAY UP THE RANKS TO *POLICE CAPTAIN* BY SECOND-GUESSING HER OWN DECISIONS.
SHE WON'T WANT TO HEAR WHAT I HAVE TO SAY.

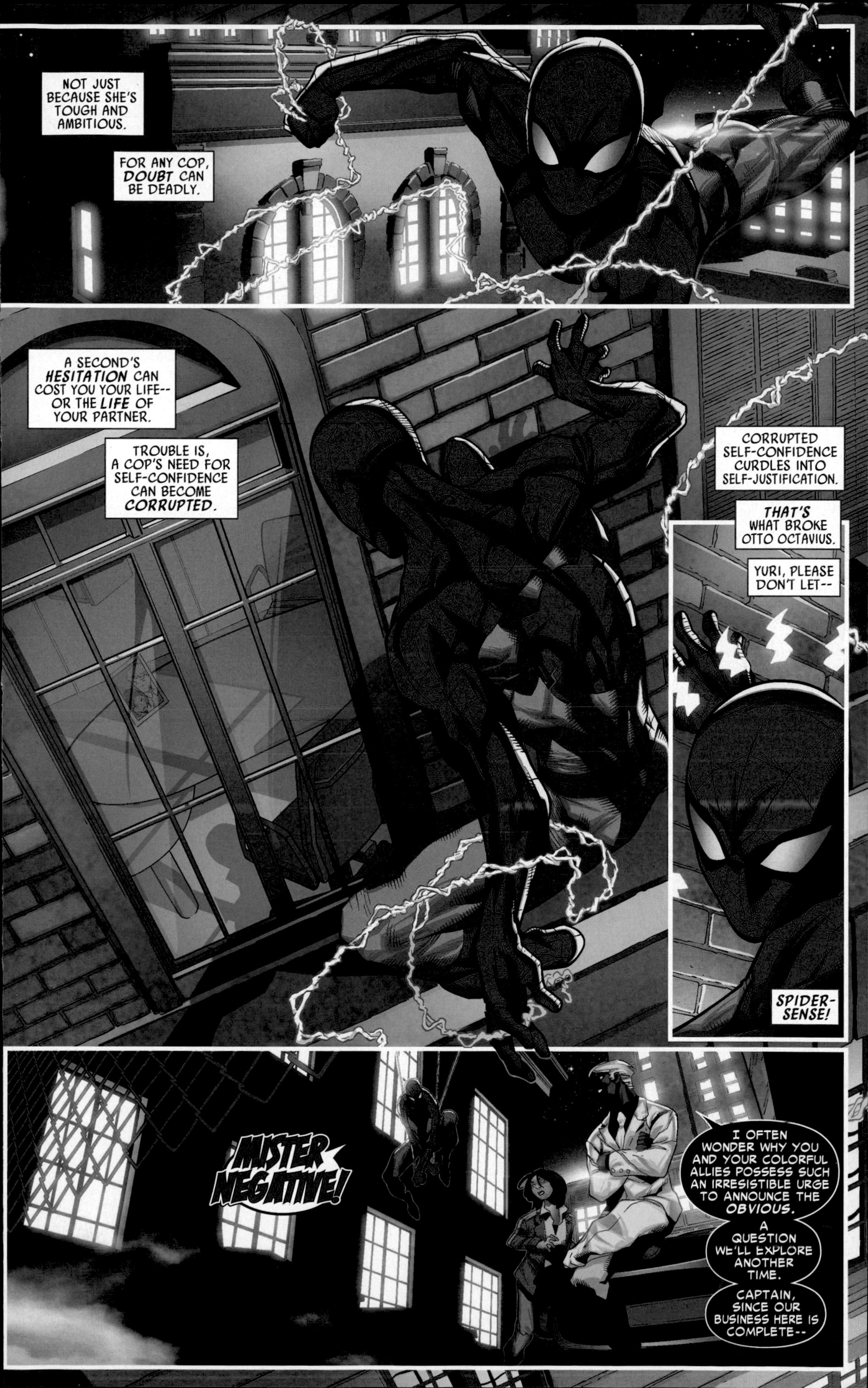
NOT JUST BECAUSE SHE'S TOUGH AND AMBITIOUS.
FOR ANY COP, DOUBT CAN BE DEADLY.
A SECOND'S HESITATION CAN COST YOU YOUR LIFE-- OR THE LIFE OF YOUR PARTNER.
TROUBLE IS, A COP'S NEED FOR SELF-CONFIDENCE CAN BECOME CORRUPTED.
CORRUPTED SELF-CONFIDENCE CURDLES INTO SELF-JUSTIFICATION.
THAT'S WHAT BROKE OTTO OCTAVIUS.
YURI, PLEASE DON'T LET--
SPIDER-SENSE!
MISTER NEGATIVE!
I OFTEN WONDER WHY YOU AND YOUR COLORFUL ALLIES POSSESS SUCH AN IRRESISTIBLE URGE TO ANNOUNCE THE OBVIOUS.
A QUESTION WE'LL EXPLORE ANOTHER TIME.
CAPTAIN, SINCE OUR BUSINESS HERE IS COMPLETE--

--I'LL SAY GOOD NIGHT.
OHNOYOUDON--

--NNNNTT‡‡
CHUNK

I HATE HOW HE DOES THAT.
HOW DOES HE DO THAT?
AND WHAT DID HE MEAN, "OUR BUSINESS IS COMPLETE"?
WHAT "BUSINESS"?
I'LL TELL YOU ON THE WAY.

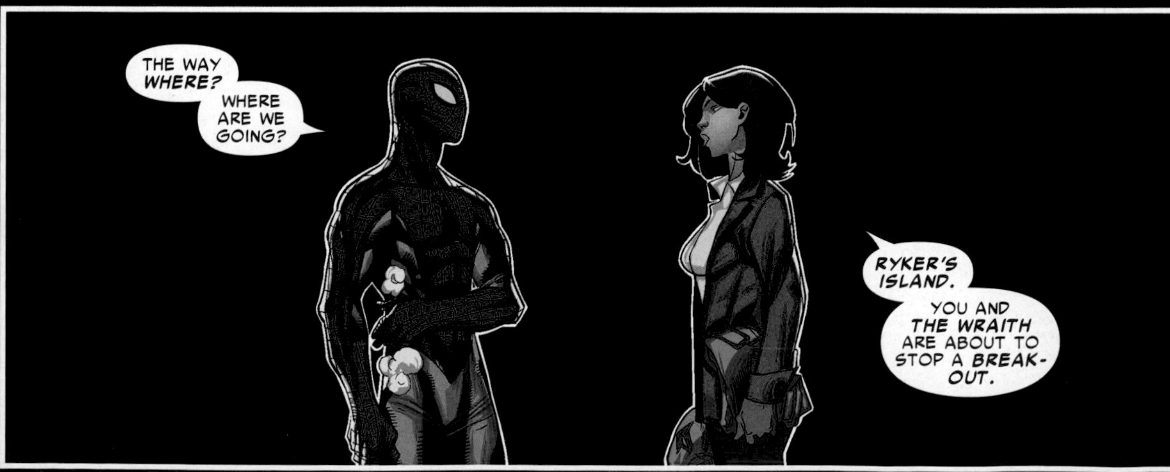
THE WAY WHERE?
WHERE ARE WE GOING?
RYKER'S ISLAND.
YOU AND THE WRAITH ARE ABOUT TO STOP A BREAK-OUT.

6:19 P.M.
THE PERIMETER GUARDS ARE ALL UNCONSCIOUS.
NEGATIVE TOLD YOU THE TRUTH. IT'S A JAILBREAK.
YOU DO REALIZE THIS IS NUTS, RIGHT?

HE'S AN INFORMANT.
HE'S PLAYING YOU.
WE'VE BEEN OVER THIS.
HE SET UP JUDGE HOWELL TO NAIL TOMBSTONE, HE HANDED YOU HAMMERHEAD--

HOWELL BROKE THE LAW. TOMBSTONE AND HAMMERHEAD ARE CRIMINALS.
I DON'T SEE HOW THE REST IS RELEVANT.
YOU DON'T-- ARE YOU KIDDING ME?

YOU'RE THE FUNNY ONE, NOT ME.
WE HAVE WORK TO DO.
SPIDER-MAN-- AND SOME WOMAN?
WHAT ARE THEY DOING HERE?

SOMEBODY SET US UP?
WHY?
WILD GUESS?
THEY WERE TIPPED OFF.
DOESN'T MATTER.
I'M TRYING TO LOOK AT ALL THIS AS A GLASS-HALF-FULL RATHER THAN A GLASS-HALF-EMPTY SITUATION.
HEY THERE, SPIDER.
WHO'S YOUR GIRLFRIEND?

TOMBSTONE IS IN SECURE QUARTERS AT THE INFIRMARY--
HAMMERHEAD IS ON THE JAIL BARGE.
LET'S GO GET THEM AND FINISH THIS.
FROM THE GLASS-HALF-FULL PERSPECTIVE--
POINT ONE:
SHE'S NOT MY GIRLFRIEND.
--WHATEVER HER CURRENT THINKING--
SHE'S AN ALLY.
--YURI WATANABE IS STILL ONE OF THE GOOD GUYS.
POINT TWO:
AS LONG AS YOU KEEP TRYING TO KILL ME--

--MY LOVE LIFE ISN'T OPEN TO DISCUSSIONNNNHH

DAMN IT, FELICIA.
YOU ALWAYS DID KNOW HOW TO GET UNDER MY SKIN.

NOW WHAT?
FELICIA AND HER PALS ARE SPLITTING UP.
MEANING IT'S CRUNCH TIME.

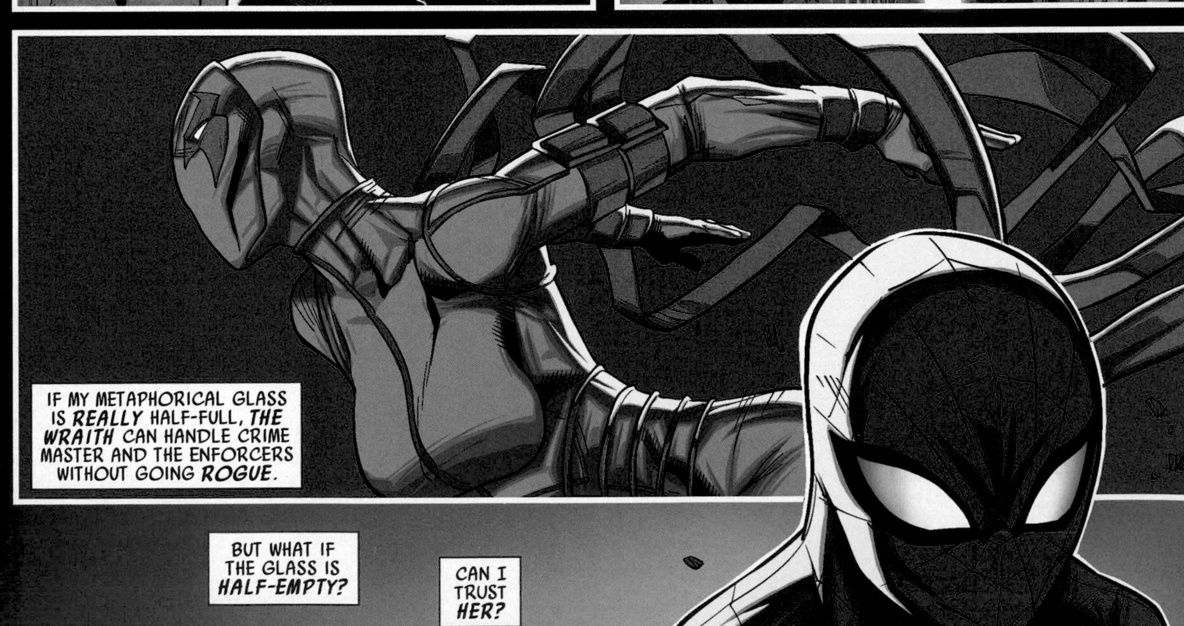
IF MY METAPHORICAL GLASS IS REALLY HALF-FULL, THE WRAITH CAN HANDLE CRIME MASTER AND THE ENFORCERS WITHOUT GOING ROGUE.
BUT WHAT IF THE GLASS IS HALF-EMPTY?
CAN I TRUST HER?

LIKE I HAVE A CHOICE.
7:01 P.M.

7:04 P.M.
SPIDER-MAN DOESN'T UNDERSTAND.
HE THINKS THERE ARE STILL RULES TO BE FOLLOWED.
WASN'T SUPPOSED TO BE LIKE THIS.

JUST A PRISON BREAK, A SIMPLE IN-AND-OUT--
--IN-AND-OUT--
OHHHGAGGAAAA
WHATSHAPPENING WHATSHAPPENING WHATSHAPPENING

FEAR GAS.
KRAK
THAK
HE THINKS THE WAY I USED TO THINK.

I KNOW YOU'RE THERE.
THE PROBLEM WITH FEAR GAS--
I CAN HEAR YOU.
--IT'S ALMOST *USELESS* IN THE OPEN AIR.

I JUST CAN'T SEE--
BUT TAKE IT INDOORS--

--SAY, INTO A CELL BLOCK *CORRIDOR*--
GNGNGHG

GET AWAY GET AWAY GET AWAY
--IT'S JUST *WONDERFUL.*

SPIDER-MAN THINKS RULES STILL MEAN MORE THAN JUSTICE.
I'VE LEARNED BETTER.
WAIT.
IS THAT--?
JUDGE HOWELL?
FIRE

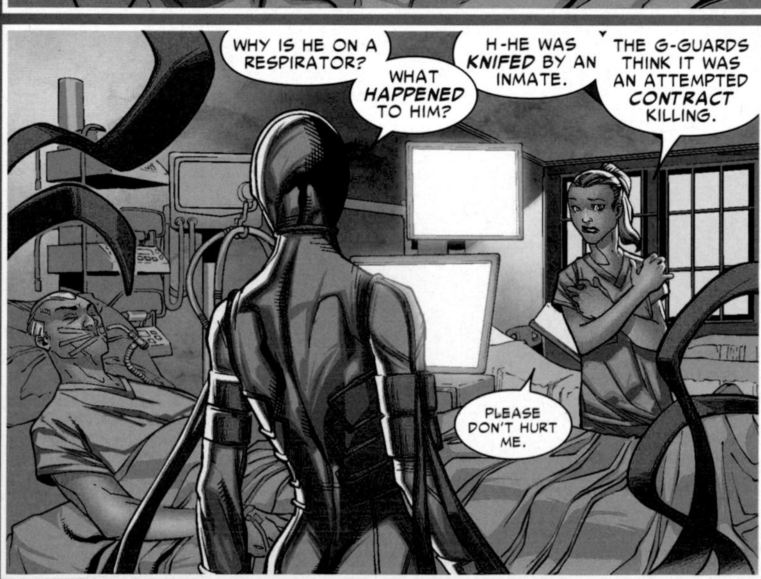
WHY IS HE ON A RESPIRATOR?
WHAT HAPPENED TO HIM?
H-HE WAS KNIFED BY AN INMATE.
THE G-GUARDS THINK IT WAS AN ATTEMPTED CONTRACT KILLING.
PLEASE DON'T HURT ME.

7:26 P.M.
I CAN HEAR CARS AND TRUCKS SCREECHING ONTO THE ISLAND OUTSIDE.
SWAT TEAMS FROM THE CITY.
FIVE MORE MINUTES AND BULLETS WILL START FLYING EVERYWHERE.
PEOPLE WILL DIE.

WE HAVE TO--
STOP!
JUST STOP, OKAY?

THERE'S AN ARMY OF COPS ON THE WAY.
IF WE KEEP THIS UP, SOMEBODY WILL GET KILLED.
I DON'T WANT IT TO BE YOU.
YOU'RE SERIOUS.
YOU EXPECT ME TO JUST... STOP AND WALK AWAY?
I KNOW YOU HATE ME NOW. YOU HAVE GOOD REASON. BUT THAT DOESN'T MATTER.

WHATEVER YOU THINK OF ME, I STILL CARE ABOUT YOU.
I BELIEVE YOU'RE A GOOD PERSON MAKING BAD CHOICES.
THIS IS YOUR CHANCE TO MAKE A GOOD ONE.
PLEASE.
THIS DOESN'T CHANGE THINGS BETWEEN US.
I NEVER THOUGHT IT WOULD.
AWW, SWEET.

YOU TWO MAKE A CUTE COUPLE.
GOT ANY GUM?
EVER SINCE I GAVE UP CIGARS I CAN'T GET ENOUGH OF THE STUFF.
DON'T MAKE ME HIT YOU.
BANG

7:29 P.M.
MAXIMUM SECURITY AREA - PROTECTIVE CUSTODY CELL BLOCK
OH NO, OH NO.
I TRUSTED YOU, YURI.
I TRUSTED YOU!

I HEARD A GUNSHOT--
WRAITH!
WHAT DID YOU DO?

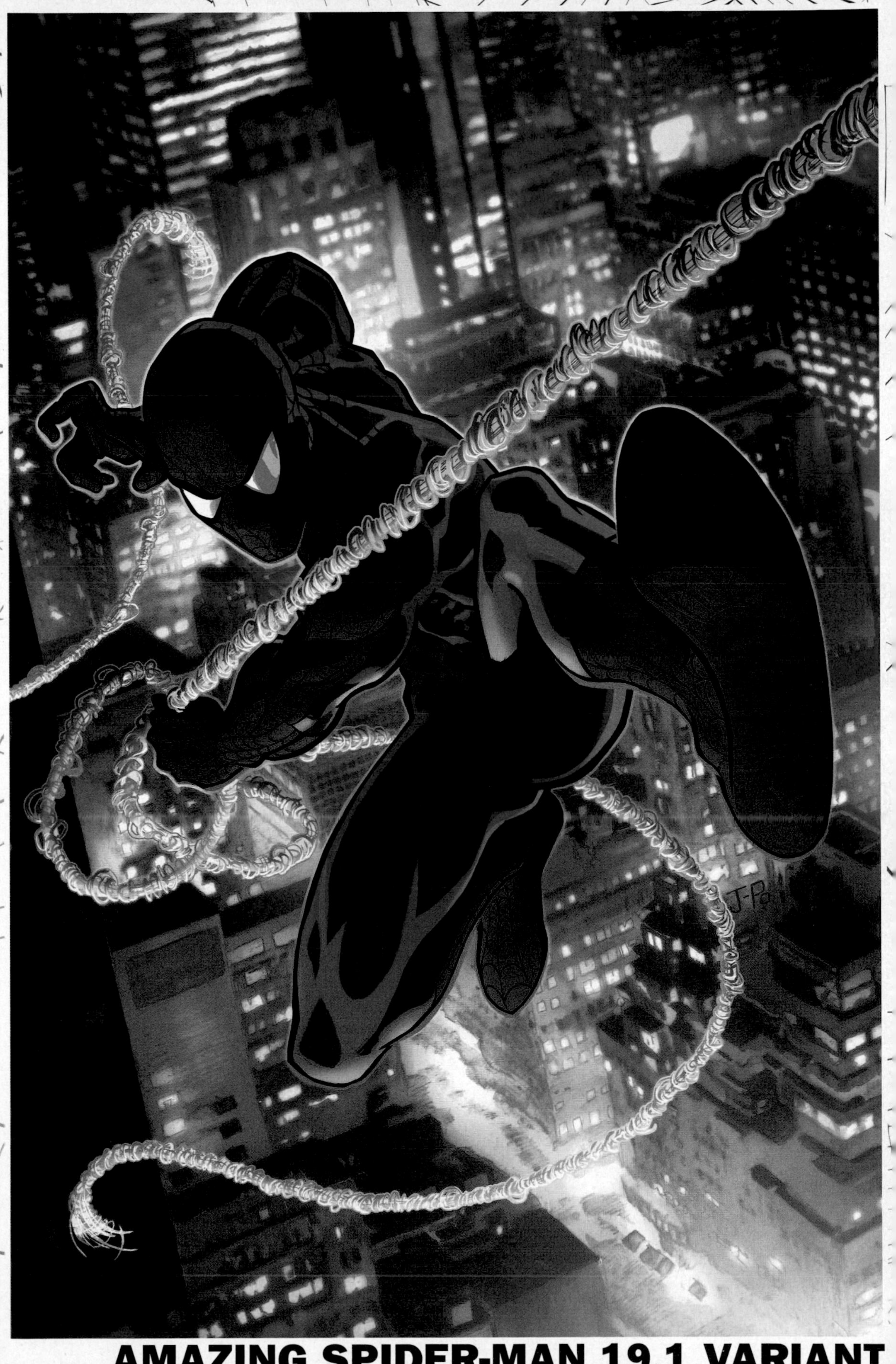

AMAZING SPIDER-MAN 19.1 VARIANT
BY JUSTIN PONSOR

AMAZING SPIDER-MAN 19.1

SPIRAL, PART FOUR

SOME MOMENTS IN LIFE ARE A *FULCRUM*.

SOMETHING *HAPPENS*.
--FOR AN ACT OF EXTRAORDINARY BRAVERY, PERFORMED IN THE LINE OF DUTY, WITH KNOWLEDGE OF THE RISK INVOLVED, AND AT IMMINENT AND PERSONAL DANGER TO HIS OWN LIFE--
--I AM PROUD TO AWARD THE *NYPD MEDAL OF HONOR* TO *SERGEANT KENNETH WATANABE*.
GRANDPA!
I'M SO PROUD OF YOU!
AH, YURIKO--
THE HONOR IS FOR THE FAMILY, NOT FOR ME.
SOMEDAY *YOU* WILL STAND HERE, AND *I'LL* BE PROUD OF YOU.

SWIK!
THE WORLD *TILTS*.
SNAP!

WHO WE ARE BEFORE THAT MOMENT--
JOHN WATANABE, YOU HAVE BEEN CONVICTED OF BRIBERY IN THE FIRST DEGREE UNDER ARTICLE 200 OF THE NEW YORK PENAL LAW, A CLASS B FELONY.
FOR ANY PUBLIC SERVANT TO ACCEPT A BRIBE IS AN AFFRONT TO CIVIC ORDER.
WHEN THAT PUBLIC SERVANT IS A POLICE OFFICER--
--THE SON OF A DECEASED, DECORATED OFFICER AND THE FATHER OF A SERVING MEMBER OF OUR ARMED FORCES--
--THE AFFRONT IS UNFORGIVABLE.
WATANABE

--AND WHO WE BECOME AFTER--
MY ANNA MARIA.
YOU... YOU REALLY LOVE HER.
YES.
AND TO SAVE HER...I MUST GIVE UP EVERY PART OF THAT LOVE.
FOR I KNOW...ONLY YOU CAN SAVE HER.
BECAUSE YOU ARE THE SUPERIOR SPIDER-MAN.

--ARE TWO DIFFERENT PEOPLE.
TTKK
TTKKKK
TTKKKK
NGH!
TEDDY!

Ryker's Island.
NOW.
I HEARD A GUNSHOT--
WRAITH!
WHAT DID YOU DO?!
I KNOW HOW THIS LOOKS.

IT LOOKS LIKE YOU JUST SHOT TOMBSTONE!
NOT ME.
ONE OF MR. NEGATIVE'S INNER DEMONS.
MASQUERADING AS THE CRIME MASTER.
DROP THE GUN!

UH, GUYS...
WE KNOW HOW THIS LOOKS.
HANDS UP BOTH OF YOU!

DON'T.

WHY DOES NOBODY EVER LISTEN TO ME?
PHTUTT
PHTOK
PHTOOM

I BELIEVE YURI.
OF COURSE I DO.
THE WRAITH DIDN'T TRY TO KILL TOMBSTONE; SHE WAS FRAMED BY MARTIN LI.
TROUBLE IS--
--EVEN IF I *DO* BELIEVE HER--

Chinatown.
--I'M NOT SURE IT MATTERS ANYMORE.
黑白
I KNOW WHO YOU ARE, *LI.*
DO YOU KNOW WHO *I* AM?

I WOULDN'T HAVE INVITED YOU FOR THIS CHAT IF I DIDN'T.
YOU WERE BORN MAYNARD TIBOLDT, AS I WAS BORN MARTIN LI.
LIKE ME, YOU CAST ASIDE THE NAME OF YOUR BIRTH AS A SNAKE SHEDS ITS SKIN.
WE ALL CHOOSE WHO WE ARE.
SO DO ME THIS COURTESY, MAYNARD:
CALL ME MR. NEGATIVE--
--AND I'LL CALL YOU RINGMASTER.
HMPH. WHAT DO YOU WANT?
TO PROPOSE AN ALLIANCE.
WITH TOMBSTONE AND HAMMERHEAD OUT OF THE PICTURE, BLACK CAT AND THE GOBLIN KING TEMPORARILY SIDELINED...
...YOU AND I ARE THE LAST MEN STANDING.
UH-UH. BACK OFF.

I KNOW ALL ABOUT YOUR CORRUPTING TOUCH.
I HAVE MY OWN METHODS OF EXERTING INFLUENCE.
YES. I'D HEARD YOU'D BEEN BLINDED.
SO PLEASED RUMORS ABOUT YOUR "RECOVERY" APPEAR JUSTIFIED.
BLACK MARKET TECH.
MY FRIENDS AND I DON'T MAKE ALLIANCES, LI.
THE *CIRCUS OF CRIME* HAS ROOM FOR ONLY ONE RINGMASTER.
HIS NAME IS *MAYNARD TIBOLDT*.

PITY A MAN WITH SUCH EXTRAORDINARY VISION CAN BE SO SHORT-SIGHTED.
LOOKS LIKE YOUR PLAN TO WIN THE CITY'S GANG WAR JUST FELL APART.
YOU THINK SO, CAPTAIN WATANABE?

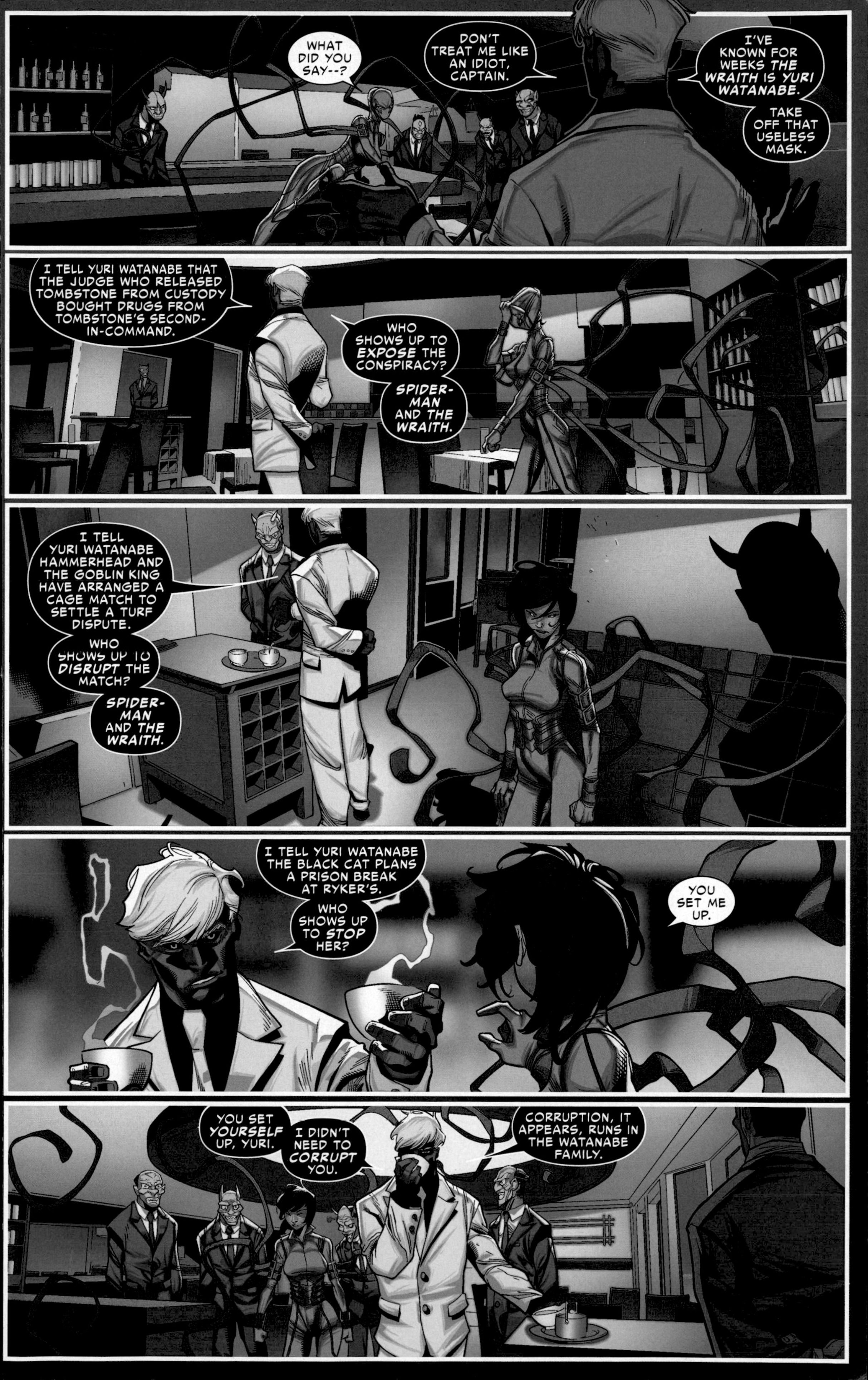
WHAT DID YOU SAY--?
DON'T TREAT ME LIKE AN IDIOT, CAPTAIN.
I'VE KNOWN FOR WEEKS THE WRAITH IS YURI WATANABE.
TAKE OFF THAT USELESS MASK.
I TELL YURI WATANABE THAT THE JUDGE WHO RELEASED TOMBSTONE FROM CUSTODY BOUGHT DRUGS FROM TOMBSTONE'S SECOND-IN-COMMAND.
WHO SHOWS UP TO EXPOSE THE CONSPIRACY?
SPIDER-MAN AND THE WRAITH.
I TELL YURI WATANABE HAMMERHEAD AND THE GOBLIN KING HAVE ARRANGED A CAGE MATCH TO SETTLE A TURF DISPUTE.
WHO SHOWS UP TO DISRUPT THE MATCH?
SPIDER-MAN AND THE WRAITH.
I TELL YURI WATANABE THE BLACK CAT PLANS A PRISON BREAK AT RYKER'S.
WHO SHOWS UP TO STOP HER?
YOU SET ME UP.
YOU SET YOURSELF UP, YURI.
I DIDN'T NEED TO CORRUPT YOU.
CORRUPTION, IT APPEARS, RUNS IN THE WATANABE FAMILY.

BASTARD!

WHAT DO YOU WANT?
NOTHING SO TERRIBLE, REALLY.
MY INNER DEMON DONALD HERE WILL KEEP AN EYE ON YOU.
THAT ALL?

JUST DO WHAT YOU'VE ALWAYS DONE, CAPTAIN.
FIGHT CRIME.
I'M EXHAUSTED.

SPENT HALF THE NIGHT LOOKING FOR YURI.
CHECKED HER APARTMENT THREE TIMES BEFORE I FINALLY HAD TO GET SOME SLEEP.
IF SHE ISN'T AT HER PRECINCT THIS MORNING--
YOU'RE DONE, CAPTAIN.
OH, THAT DOESN'T SOUND GOOD.
WORD CAME FROM RYKER'S ISLAND THIS MORNING.
JUDGE HOWELL DIED AN HOUR AGO.
I KNEW HE'D BEEN STABBED--
THIS IS ON YOU.
I ORDERED YOU TO TAKE IT SLOW WITH HOWELL. TO BE SURE. GO BY THE BOOK.
YOU DIDN'T LISTEN.
NOW A JUDGE...NOT A COP, BUT PART OF THE FAMILY...
...IS DEAD BECAUSE YOU MADE IT PERSONAL.
YOU'RE FINISHED IN THIS DEPARTMENT, WATANABE.
YOU'LL KEEP YOUR JOB, BUT YOUR CAREER IS OVER.
BAD TIME TO TALK?

ALL I EVER TRIED TO DO WAS PROTECT MY PRECINCT AND TAKE DOWN THE BAD GUYS.
THAT'S WHAT YOU TELL YOURSELF.
IT'S TRUE.
IS IT?
YOU MADE A MISTAKE, YURI.

DON'T MAKE THINGS WORSE BY DENYING IT.

I KNOW WHAT I DID, SPIDER-MAN.

WHATEVER COMES NEXT...
...I CAN LIVE WITH IT.
NOT THE REPLY I WANTED TO HEAR.

THE YURI WATANABE I KNEW WAS A PASSIONATE COP AND A RELUCTANT VIGILANTE.
THIS WOMAN--
I'M NOT SURE WHO SHE IS.
ABOUT TIME YOU DECIDED TO SHOW YOURSELF.
YOU KNOW I'M KEEPING AN EYE ON YOU, RIGHT?

REALLY? I HADN'T NOTICED.
SO, WHY ARE WE AT THE CONVENTION CENTER?
ANOTHER HOT TIP FROM YOUR PAL MR. NEGATIVE?

YOU WANT TO PICK A FIGHT OR TAKE DOWN SOME BAD GUYS?
WHAT, WE CAN'T DO BOTH?
SIGH
OKAY, I'LL BITE.
WHICH BAD GUYS ARE WE TAKING DOWN TONIGHT?
KRAK
K-KRAK
KRAK

EMPIRE STATE
CENTER
1C
3 - 3E
rystal Palace, Galleria
, 1E, 2D
od Court
THE CIRCUS OF CRIME!
THESE GUYS?
I HATE THESE GUYS.

NEW YOR
TECH FAI
THWIP
HUH?
UH-OH--
I THINK THE CIRCUS EXPRESSION YOU'RE GROPING FOR WHEN SEEKING AID FROM FELLOW CARNIES IS, "HEY, RUBE!"
WHOOPS, TOO LATE.

AND YOU.
HASN'T ANYONE EVER TOLD YOU THERE'S A SIMPLE TREATMENT FOR ACID REFLUX?
ASK YOUR DOCTOR WHEN YOU SEE HIM.
FWOOSH
KRASH
I'M GUESSING THAT WILL BE REAL SOON.

GONNA CATCH YOU.
GONNA SQUISH YOU.

GONNA--
--WOOO-WOOO-WOOO--
ONE BLAST FROM MY SONIC AIR HORN AND THE LAUGH'S ON YOU, SPIDER-MAN!

WOOO-WOOO--
ULP.

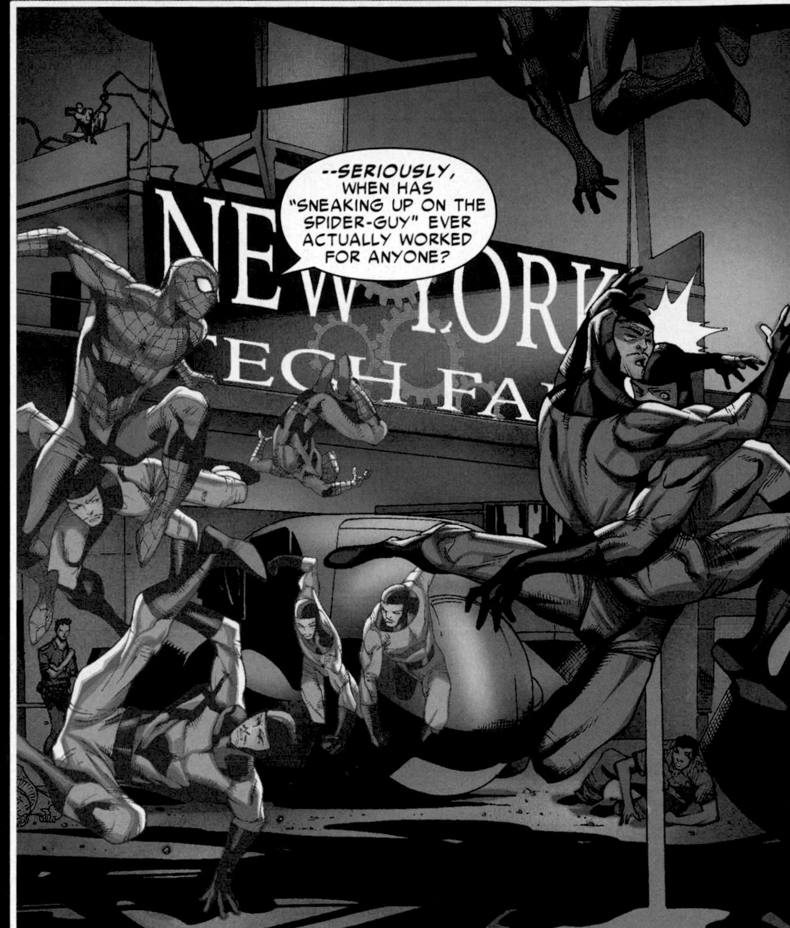

BUT IF THIS *IS* A GAME--

--I'M DONE PLAYING BY EVERYONE ELSE'S RULES.
CLAP
CLAP
CLAP
BRAVO, WEB-SLINGER.
A MOST IMPRESSIVE DISPLAY OF ATHLETIC SKILL AND DERRING-DO.
YET, LIKE THE GORMLESS IDIOTS WHO WANDER THESE HALLS MERELY TO MARVEL AT THE SPECTACULAR DISPLAYS OF OVERSIZED GADGETS AND GIZMOS--
--YOU MISTAKE THE SIDESHOW FOR THE MAIN ACT.
ALL THESE ENORMOUS PROPS ARE A DISTRACTION.
NOT FOLLOWING THE METAPHOR HERE.
FROM WHAT?
"THE ONE ITEM OF MONETARY VALUE AT THIS SHOW HONORING THE EXCESSES OF OUR TECHNOPHILIC SOCIETY.
"A WATCH."

DID YOU SAY A WATCH?
THE MOST VALUABLE WATCH IN HISTORY.
A HIGH-TECH PROTOTYPE, PURE GOLD WITH A DIAMOND FACE.
INSURED FOR TEN MILLION DOLLARS.
HUH.
I SEE WHAT YOU MEAN BY THE "EXCESS" REMARK.
STILL DON'T ENTIRELY GET THE SIDESHOW METAPHOR.
THEN LET ME CLARIFY.
MY CIRCUS ALLIES WERE THE SIDESHOW...
...I'M THE RINGMASTER!
LESSON LEARNED:
TOP HAT, TAILS, AND JODHPURS MAKE YOU LOOK LIKE A JOKE.
PEOPLE THINK YOU'RE A JOKE, THEY DROP THEIR GUARD.
AND JUST LIKE THAT...

...NOBODY'S LAUGHING ANYMORE.
I CAN'T FIGHT THESE GUARDS.
THEY'RE NOT RESPONSIBLE FOR WHAT THEY'RE DOING.
THEY DON'T HAVE A CHOICE.
SPTAK
SPTOOF
SPAFF

I DO.
I CAN PICK MY ENEMIES.

I CAN MAKE THE RIGHT MOVE.

I CAN DO THE RIGHT THING.
THWIPP

BECAUSE, WITH GREAT POWER...
AH, HECK.
SPLORTCH
WHO AM I KIDDING?
GLMPHHFF

SOMETIMES IT JUST FEELS GOOD TO PUNCH SOMEBODY.

AGRRGHH
I HAVE NO CHOICE.

MR. NEGATIVE PLAYED ME, JUST AS SPIDER-MAN WARNED ME HE WOULD.
THANKS TO HIM, I CAN'T BE A COP ANYMORE.
THANKS TO HIM, YURI WATANABE'S LIFE IS OVER.

BUT THAT DOESN'T MEAN HE OWNS ME.

THAT DOESN'T MEAN I CAN'T DESTROY HIM.

YURI WATANABE IS DEAD.

THE WRAITH LIVES...
...AND SHE WANTS JUSTICE.

AMAZING SPIDER-MAN 20.1 VARIANT
BY NICK BRADSHAW & JIM CAMPBELL

AMAZING SPIDER-MAN 20.1

SPIRAL, PART FIVE

The Third Precinct.
9:33 A.M.
EVERYBODY BACK!
THIS IS OUR SCORE!
YOU'RE ON HAMMERHEAD'S TURF, FREAK.
HIS TURF, OUR MONEY!
POLICE! ALL OF YOU, GUNS DOWN AND HANDS UP--
THIS IS BAD.

The Third Precinct.
10:42 A.M.
TOLD YOU TAKING DOWN THIS ARMORED CAR WOULD BE A CINCH.
DIDN'T MENTION THERE'D BE COPS.
THAT A PROBLEM?
WITH KINGPIN OUT OF THE PICTURE, THERE ARE NO PROBLEMS, MATE--
--ONLY POSSIBILITIES.
POLICE! BOTH OF YOU, HANDS UP--
REALLY BAD.

The Third Precinct.
12:18 P.M.
GRAB EVERY BOX!
THESE DRUGS ARE WORTH A FORTUNE ON THE BLACK MARKET!
POLICE! ALL OF YOU--
REALLY--
REALLY BAD!
COPS COMING! WHAT DO WE DO?
IS THAT A SERIOUS QUESTION?
ANYBODY GETS IN YOUR WAY--KILL THEM!

1:07 P.M.
EVER SINCE DOC OCK USED HIS "SUPERIOR" SKILLS TO LOCK DOWN CRIME A FEW MONTHS BACK--
--PARTS OF THIS CITY HAVE BEEN A PROVERBIAL POWDER KEG--
--JUST BEGGING FOR AN ARSONIST TO LIGHT THINGS UP.
1:29 P.M.
RIVAL GANGS, LONE WOLVES, COSTUMED CRAZIES--
MAYBE IT'S A MIRACLE THE WHOLE MESS DIDN'T EXPLODE SOONER.
1:58 P.M.
BUT WHY NOW?
WHY ALL AT ONCE?
WHY TODAY?

2:02 P.M.
OH, DON'T BE NAIVE.
THIS WHOLE GANG WAR IS YOUR FAULT.
MY FAULT?
WOOF!

YOU CAN'T PUT THIS ON ME, FELICIA-- I'M TRYING TO STOP THE CRAZY!
ONLY MY FRIENDS GET TO CALL ME FELICIA.
FINE.
YOU'RE THE BLACK CAT, I'M YOUR FRIENDLY NEIGHBORHOOD SPIDER-MAN.

STILL DON'T SEE HOW THIS IS MY FAU-- OWWW!
I'LL MAKE IT SIMPLE FOR YOU.
SWISSKKK

THE THIRD PRECINCT'S GANG STRUCTURE WAS THE CRIMINAL EQUIVALENT OF A JENGA PUZZLE.
WHEN YOU AND YOUR NEW GIRLFRIEND BUSTED TOMBSTONE--
--AND FOLLOWED UP BY BRINGING DOWN HIS RIVAL HAMMERHEAD--

--YOU PULLED ONE TOO MANY PIECES OUT OF THE STACK.
THANK YOU.
FIRST OF ALL, THAT'S ACTUALLY A PRETTY GOOD METAPHOR.
SECOND OF ALL, THE WRAITH IS NOT MY "GIRLFRIEND."

WHATEVER.
POINT IS, YOU AND YOUR LITTLE PAL HAVE DONE ME A FAVOR.
CHAOS IS THE MOTHER OF OPPORTUNITY.

ONCE THE DUST SETTLES I'LL PICK THROUGH THE RUBBLE FOR THE SHINY BITS.
UNLESS HE AND HIS *INNER DEMONS* GET THERE FIRST.

FELICIA, *PLEASE,* DON'T MAKE ME HUR--
RKKK
I SAID--
YOU.
DON'T.
CALL.
ME.
FELICIA!

HARD TO BELIEVE WE USED TO BE MORE THAN FRIENDS.
SOME PEOPLE, WHEN THEY DECIDE YOU BETRAYED THEM, EVEN IF IT WASN'T YOU BUT SOME MAD DOCTOR WHO HIJACKED YOUR HEAD--
THEY NEVER FORGET. NEVER FORGIVE.

ONE OF THESE DAYS I'LL HAVE TO FIGHT BACK.
BUT NOT TODAY.
TODAY I'VE GOT BUSINESS WITH THE *"HE"* FELICIA MENTIONED...

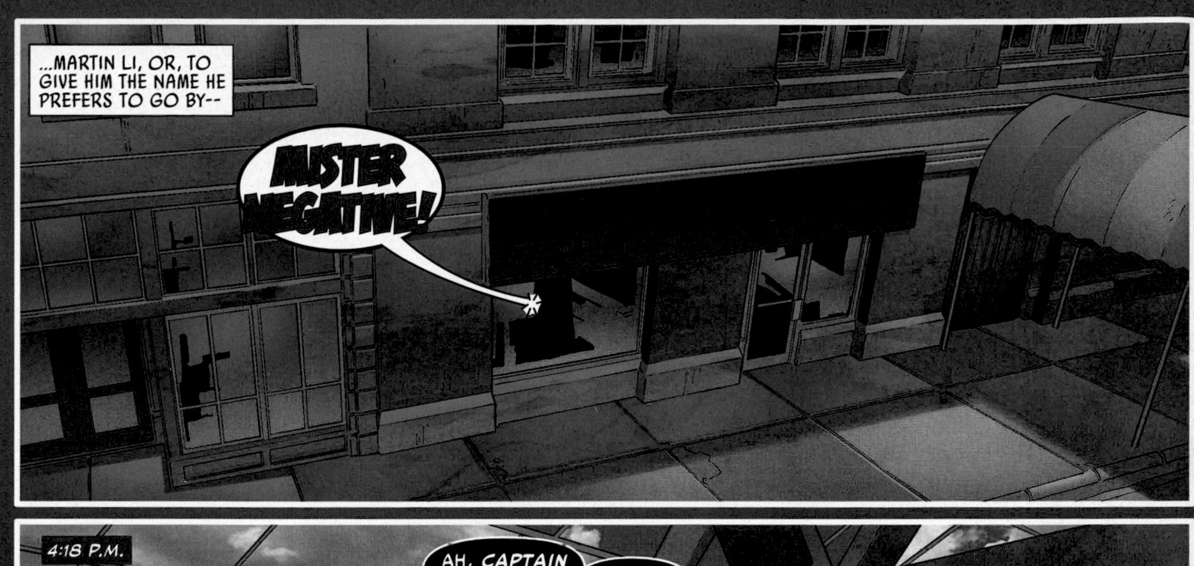
...MARTIN LI, OR, TO GIVE HIM THE NAME HE PREFERS TO GO BY--
MISTER NEGATIVE!

4:18 P.M.
AH, CAPTAIN WATANABE--
I WAS WONDERING WHEN YOU'D JOIN US.
I'D HAVE SENT ONE OF MY INNER DEMONS TO INVITE YOU TO THE PARTY--
--BUT AS YOU CAN SEE, THEY'VE BEEN BUSY.
EVERYTHING HAPPENING IN THE THIRD PRECINCT--
THAT'S YOUR DOING?
NOT ENTIRELY.

MY INNER DEMONS STRUCK THE SPARK, BUT YOU PILED THE TINDER.
SPEAKING OF MY DEMONS-- WHERE'S DONALD? HE FAILED TO REPORT ON YOUR ADVENTURE LAST NIGHT.
I HOPE NOTHING HAPPENED TO HIM.

SOMETHING DID.
I KILLED HIM.
WHAT DID YOU SAY?
I. KILLED. HIM.
MORE TO THE POINT--
I'M GOING TO KILL YOU.
"STOP" ME?
PTOOF
FTOOM
PTOOM
PTOOFF

YOU'RE "MISTER NEGATIVE"-- YOU CORRUPT PEOPLE.
THUNK

YOU THINK CORRUPTION IS CONTROL.
IT ISN'T.

AND YOU CAN'T STOP WHAT YOU CAN'T CONTROL.
KRUNCH

THWAP
WHO ARE YOU TRYING TO CONVINCE?
THE GUY WHO'S ALREADY LEFT THE BUILDING--

--OR YOURSELF?
SPIDER-MAN.
WHY ARE YOU HERE?
WHY WON'T YOU LEAVE ME ALONE?

BECAUSE I HAVEN'T GIVEN UP ON YOU.
I STILL THINK YOU CAN CHANGE THE PATH YOU'VE BEEN FOLLOWING.
WHAT IF I DON'T *WANT* TO CHANGE?
I DON'T BELIEVE THAT.
I *CAN'T* BELIEVE THAT.
THE YURI WATANABE I KNOW--

THE YURI WATANABE *YOU* KNOW?

SHE WASN'T REAL.
THAT YURI WAS A STORY I MADE UP, A LIE I TOLD MYSELF--THE GOOD GRANDDAUGHTER I THOUGHT I WANTED TO BE.

DO YOU KNOW WHAT A *WRAITH* IS, SPIDER-MAN?
IT'S A WISP, A TRACE, A *GHOST*--
--THE FADING MEMORY OF SOMEONE WHO'S *GONE*.

THERE'S A REASON I TOOK THE MASK BACK SO EASILY AFTER GIVING IT UP.
I DIDN'T UNDERSTAND THAT FULLY UNTIL I KILLED A MAN LAST NIGHT.

YURI WATANABE WOULD HAVE BEEN *HORRIFIED* BY WHAT I DID.
YURI, PLEASE--
BUT YOU KNOW HOW *I* FELT?

PTOOM
PTOOM
I FELT FREE!
KRAKK
PTOOM
NGNGH
PTOOM

I SAW THAT COMING.
I SAW IT COMING BUT I COULDN'T, WOULDN'T BELIEVE IT.

SO I GUESS YURI WATANABE ISN'T THE ONLY ONE WHO HAS TO FACE AN UNPLEASANT FACT ABOUT THEMSELVES.
FELICIA, YURI...
SOMETIMES WHAT I WANT TO BELIEVE BLINDS ME TO THE TRUTH ABOUT PEOPLE.

SOMETIMES I CAN'T SEE THE MIRROR THROUGH THE SMOKE.
WAIT.
PLEASE.
GIVE ME A CHANCE...
TO DO WHAT?

THIS!
I USED TO WONDER HOW MARTIN LI'S CORRUPTING TOUCH MANAGED TO AFFECT EVERYONE HE USED IT ON.
WOULDN'T THERE HAVE TO BE SOMEBODY, SOMEWHERE, HE COULDN'T CORRUPT?
I DON'T THINK I REALIZED, TILL JUST NOW--

DARKNESS WAITS IN ALL OF US.
GETTING YOU OUT OF HERE.
DON'T NEED YOUR HELP--
NOT ABOUT YOU.
YOU'RE BEYOND SAVING.
THEY'RE NOT!

WHAT YOU'VE DONE IS *YOUR* FAULT--
--BUT I PLAYED A PART IN THIS TOO.
I CHOSE NOT TO SEE WHAT YOU WERE BECOMING.
IF I'D FACED THE TRUTH--
--MAYBE I COULD'VE *HELPED* YOU.
SO THAT'S ON ME.
THE REST OF IT, THOUGH--
--LIKE YOUR *CHIEF* SAID, YURI--

THAT'S ON YOU!
WHAMM
WOW.
GUESS I WAS HOLDING BACK MORE ANGER THAN I THOUGHT.
I SHOULDN'T FEEL AS GOOD ABOUT THIS AS I DO.
BUT I DO FEEL PRETTY GOOD.
DARKNESS REALLY DOES WAIT INSIDE US ALL.

5:19 P.M.
INNER DEMONS... GONE...
...JUST NEED TO... REGROUP...
...SIMPLE... SETBACK...

YOU AND I MUST HAVE DIFFERENT DEFINITIONS OF THE WORD "SETBACK," MARTY.
NOOOO...

SIGH

SOME GUYS NEVER GET THE MEMO.
SOME GUYS DON'T READ THE MEMO.
TELL ME, MARTY...

...WHICH GUY ARE YOU?

5:26 P.M.
THE ONLY GOOD THING ABOUT MISTER NEGATIVE'S CORRUPTING TOUCH IS THAT IT'S TEMPORARY.
5:36 P.M.
ONCE THE FIRES SET BY HIS INNER DEMONS BURN OUT, THE THIRD PRECINCT WILL RETURN TO NORMAL...
5:49 P.M.
...OR AS "NORMAL" AS THINGS EVER GET IN THIS CITY.
NOT A VERY HIGH BAR TO MEET, I ADMIT.
5:58 P.M.
MAYBE THERE'S NO SUCH THING AS "NORMAL."
THE WORLD KEEPS CHANGING.
NOTHING STAYS THE SAME.

THE WORLD TURNS, PEOPLE TURN, EVERYTHING TURNS.
AND IT NEVER STOPS.

WHAT CAN YOU SAY?
IT'S THE CIRCLE OF LIFE.

BUT IT ISN'T A CIRCLE. NOT REALLY.
IT'S A *SPIRAL*.
THE THING ABOUT SPIRALS?

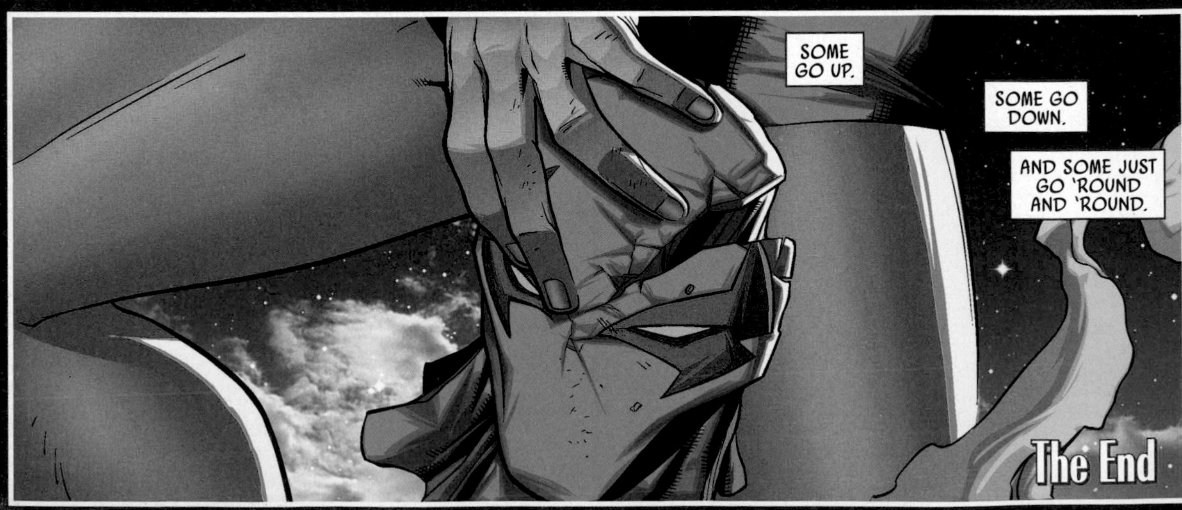
SOME GO UP.
SOME GO DOWN.
AND SOME JUST GO 'ROUND AND 'ROUND.
The End